Occupational Guidance

Power Plant Engineer

Description of Work

Utility companies that provide light, power, and heat for communities are located throughout the United States. Some power plants are municipally owned and serve the needs of the immediate community. Other plants are large generating facilities that serve a designated section of the country. Power Plant Engineers direct power-generating stations and some substations. These professionals help design, evaluate, construct, and maintain plants, systems, and equipment.

Power Plant Engineers may have a variety of responsibilities. In small companies, one person or a small group of people may handle all of these responsibilities. Engineers in large companies typically specialize in a single area of this work.

Engineers who specialize in power supply planning try to prepare for future operations and power needs. They evaluate projections about electricity use and the company's abilities to meet those projections. They then determine if, when, and where the company should expand or build new facilities. These professionals need to consider the cost and reliability of maintenance and construction, as well as the environmental and social effects expansions may have.

Individuals who work with plant engineering and construction handle the tasks involved in constructing new plants or modifying existing structures. They need to make sure plants are safe and efficient and that the facilities follow environmental regulations. These engineers may work on the construction of nuclear, coal burning, hydroelectric, gas turbine, or diesel peaking plants. They interact with building contractors. They also manage the licensing, procurement, testing, and start-up activities of the plant.

In addition to power plants, individuals may work at substations, which contain the equipment and machinery that switch, transform, or regulate the voltage of plant systems. These substations link power plants, transmission lines, and distribution lines. Substation engineers are responsible for overseeing a new substation, from its design to its operation. They may be responsible for making cost estimates, conducting application studies, determining specifications, collecting bids, and coordinating the work of a variety of suppliers and departments. Substation engineers also work with major power-handling equipment like circuit breakers, transformers, conductor arrangements, and structures.

Individuals who specialize as transmission engineers design the overhead high-voltage transmission lines that connect power plants, substations, and neighboring utilities. They also design the underground lines that many communities in metropolitan areas use. These professionals prepare budget estimates, select line routes, conduct studies, coordinate and supervise the preparation of construction drawings, and specify construction materials. They work with other people to keep each project on schedule and within its budget. They also make sure the project conforms to state and federal regulations.

Most power plants prioritize the need to inspect, test, and repair their facilities. These plants typically staff a department to manage protection and electrical maintenance activities. The department employees test and repair electrical equipment like transformers, breakers, and regulators. They may also repair sophisticated protection and control equipment. Power Plant Engineers who work in such departments conduct engineering studies and make sure power lines and substations are operating safely and correctly.

Some engineers specialize in testing activities. These individuals perform tests in laboratories and in the field to make sure power plants are operating safely and efficiently. They also make sure the levels of air and water emissions meet government standards. These professionals may analyze coal and oil samples, boiler water, and groundwater, as well as test construction materials.

Power Plant Engineers can also work in the area of power distribution and service. Individuals who specialize in this area study new housing and industry. They try to determine the future needs of these developments and advise the company about the design, building, and maintenance of distribution facilities. The engineers may dispatch and supervise repair employees during storms. They may also work with electricity-use control devices to encourage the

GOE 05.06.01/O*Net 95021

O*Net-Soc 51-8013.01

conservation of energy during periods that experience the greatest demand. In addition, these professionals may help create service policies and standards. They often work with customers.

Some engineers specialize in research. They analyze, develop, apply, and demonstrate new and improved energy technologies. Researchers may focus on solar power, energy conservation, unconventional fuels, and other aspects of power generation and use.

Individuals who are interested in this profession may also want to read about related careers, including Wastewater Treatment Plant Operator (*Occupational Guidance* Vol. VIII, Unit 1I, No. 5), Electrical & Electronics Engineer (Vol. VII, Unit 3H, No. 7), and Mechanical Engineer (Vol. IV, Unit 5H, No. 19). Other engineering positions are listed in the *Occupational Guidance* Cluster Index under the classification 05.01 Engineering.

People who are interested in a career in engineering technology may want to read about the occupations of Civil Engineering Technician (*Occupational Guidance* Vol. V, Unit 4H, No. 12) and Mechanical Engineering Technician (Vol. IV, Unit 4H, No. 2).

Earnings

Power Plant Engineers' earnings vary according to their level of education and experience and the size and location of the plant at which they work. Small power facilities that serve a mostly rural area may pay entry-level engineers from $48,000 to $55,000 a year. Large plants in urban areas generally pay engineers a starting salary of about $50,000 or more annually. Most professionals in this field earn between $55,000 and $78,000 a year. Experienced individuals may earn more than $85,000 a year.

Employers typically offer benefits to full-time professionals in this field. Power Plant Engineers may receive health insurance, sick leave, paid vacation time, and retirement benefits. They may also receive bonus pay for working on holidays.

History of Occupation

People in ancient societies applied principles of engineering. For example, the Egyptian people who lived in the Nile River Valley more than 5,000 years ago used a water screw for irrigation. They also used inclined planes to build the pyramids. Societies started to understand electricity and other power sources at a much later time.

The amount of scientific and technical knowledge in the 1700s and 1800s grew rapidly. As a result, individuals started to specialize in certain areas of engineering and training programs developed for engineers.

In the 17th century, Dr. Thomas Browne became the first person to write the word electricity in a book. In the 1750s, Benjamin Franklin performed experiments with a kite and a conducting string. Through these experiments, he proved that lightning is identical to electricity.

Alessandro Volta, from whose name the word volt was derived, made the first electric battery. In the 1830s, Michael Faraday discovered that a magnetic force in motion produces an electrical current. Faraday found that one current could induce another in a different circuit. His discovery is the principle of the transformer. Oersted, Ampere, and Maxwell also contributed to developments in this field during the late 18th and early 19th centuries. The Centennial Exposition of 1876, which was held in Philadelphia, helped promote the development of new uses of electricity. At this exposition, inventors and companies exhibited devices such as telegraphs, batteries, telephones, bells, and generators.

In 1882, Thomas A. Edison directed the operation of the first plants to generate electricity. In that same year, steam-powered engines appeared in London, England, and in New York City. In Appleton, Wisconsin, a water turbine that generated electricity was developed. The capacities of these early plants were fractions of the kilowatt power that present-day facilities generate.

By the late 19th century, factories, shops, and homes started to use electricity. Electrical engineers applied this technology to streetcars, elevators, and electric motors. In the 20th century, engineers developed new ways to generate and store power. Instead of a plant being cluttered with belts and shafts, each machine could have its own motor.

The profession of electrical engineering developed with the discovery of electrical power. Two years after Thomas Edison started operating the first power generating plant, the American Institute of Electrical Engineers was founded. Edison was one of the founding members.

Present-day power companies continue to rely on the principles of engineering. They hire Power Plant Engineers to maintain plants, stations, and substations and to plan for the future.

Working Conditions

Power Plant Engineers typically spend most of their time in their offices or in power plants. Individuals who are responsible for supervising new installations or managing new power applications frequently work on location. They often interact with people ranging from customers to plant employees. Engineers typically have comfortable office environments. Power plant conditions may be hot, noisy, and dirty, however.

Hours of Work

Most engineers in this field regularly work forty hours per week. They may not work standard shifts, however. Power plants are continuously in operation. Therefore, individuals may need to work nights, weekends, and holidays at times.

Ability Required

Power Plant Engineers need to be interested in and have an aptitude for applied science, electrical and mechanical engineering, and mathematics. These individuals should be able to analyze problems and develop solutions. They should also be able to clearly express ideas verbally and in writing. Engineers need to be able to visualize ideas in three dimensions. By looking at a blueprint, they should be able to envision the different parts of a machine. In addition, these professionals need to have computer skills.

Temperament Required

Engineers should be self-confident, patient, and persistent in their work. They should be self-motivated and take initiative in putting ideas into action. These individuals should work well with others. They should be comfortable serving in a supervisory role and making decisions. Power Plant Engineers can benefit from being creative, especially when they need to develop solutions to problems.

Education and Training Required

Prospective engineers need to obtain a minimum of a bachelor's degree. Some power plants prefer to hire candidates who majored in electrical or nuclear engineering during their undergraduate studies. They may consider hiring applicants who have a civil, industrial, mechanical, chemical, or metallurgical engineering degree, however. Many employers also prefer to hire candidates who have a master's degree. Individuals usually spend from four to five years completing the courses necessary for a bachelor's degree in engineering. They often spend an additional two years earning a master's degree.

During their undergraduate studies, prospective Power Plant Engineers may take classes in the principles of electrical engineering, electrical circuits, electric power systems, computer and industrial electronics, transistor circuits, electromagnetic fields and waves, and engineering thermodynamics. In addition, they often take courses in physics, chemistry, metallurgy, electrical generation, and methods of heat transfer.

Once individuals have completed their degree, they can apply for entry-level engineering positions in power plants. As they gain experience, these professionals may have opportunities to advance to positions of increased responsibility. Most employers provide intensive on-the-job training for engineers. For some positions, individuals may need to pass annual examinations.

Finances Required Before Earning

Prospective engineers need to obtain a minimum of a bachelor's degree. At public home-state universities, undergraduate tuition often costs from $6,000 to $16,000 a year. Students from out of state may pay additional fees. Private colleges frequently charge from $15,000 to more than $30,000 a year for undergraduate tuition. Students should also budget for living expenses, which can range from $5,000 to $15,000 annually. Books and supplies may cost about $1,000 each year.

Individuals who decide to pursue a master's degree after they obtain their bachelor's degree need to attend graduate school. Graduate-level tuition usually costs about the same as or slightly more than undergraduate tuition. Many graduate students work as teaching or research assistants to offset the costs of their education.

Financial Aid Information

Engineering societies, associations, and schools may offer scholarships for students in this field. Schools may offer scholarships that cover all or part of the recipients' tuition expenses. These scholarships may be renewable from year to year. Individuals should check with the financial aid office of the school they plan to or currently attend for more information about such aid.

For a free booklet on financial aid, one may write to or e-mail the following:

Financial Aids for Students
Finney Company
3943 Meadowbrook Road
Minneapolis, Minnesota 55426-4505
feedback@finney-hobar.com

Attractive Features

Power Plant Engineers typically have comfortable office environments and a high level of job security. Many individuals in this profession gain a sense of satisfaction in feeling that they are helping to provide electrical power for their communities. Engineers may also appreciate the challenges that accompany this career and the opportunities to use different skills and creativity.

Disadvantages

Power plants need to operate continuously, so engineers may have to work some evening, night, or weekend hours. Some people in this profession find that their schedule disrupts their personal or social life. Engineers may occasionally feel frustrated with a project's rate of progress. Some people are discouraged from entering this career by its educational requirements.

Outlook for the Future

The demand for power generation in the United States continues to grow as the population increases. Factors such as utility deregulation and foreign competition have slowed job growth in this industry, however. Despite the slowed growth, power companies continue to rely on Power Plant Engineers to design and develop power systems and equipment and refurbish old systems. Individuals who have strong academic credentials and some experience will likely find employment opportunities. Some jobs should become available as current engineers advance to management positions or retire from the workforce.

Licensing, Unions, Organizations

Engineers can choose to join a number of professional and technical societies, including the American Society of Mechanical Engineers, the National Society of Professional Engineers, and the Institute of Electrical and Electronics Engineers. Many Power Plant Engineers also become members of the National Association of Power Engineers. Some individuals in this profession join unions, such as the International Brotherhood of Electrical Workers or the Utility Workers Union of America.

After they gain experience in this field, professionals may choose to register with their state boards. The National Council of Examiners for Engineering and Surveying sponsors the registration program.

Suggested Courses in High School

Students who plan to enter engineering schools should take college-preparatory classes, including courses in mathematics, science, English, a foreign language, and social studies. They should emphasize mathematics and science classes, like calculus, algebra, plane geometry, trigonometry, solid geometry, physics, and chemistry, in their curriculum. Prospective engineers can develop their communication skills through composition and speech classes. They can also benefit from taking courses in computers and information science. Through industrial technology classes, students may be able to develop technical and mechanical or electrical skills.

Suggested High School Activities

By participating in various extracurricular activities and organizations, like student government, science and mathematics clubs, and a speech or debate team, students can learn to take initiative and develop leadership abilities. They can start learning about engineering by joining the Junior Engineering Technical Society (JETS). Individuals can also develop applicable skills for this career by participating in local or state science fairs. They can create an engineering project to enter into these competitions.

Methods to Enter Work

Most colleges have placement offices that can help graduates find a position in this field. Professional organizations may also offer placement services for members. Companies that are interested in hiring graduates may send representatives to college campuses. These representatives may then interview prospective employees. Some employers advertise employment opportunities through professional journals, on the Internet, or in the classified sections of newspapers. In addition, candidates can apply directly to companies for which they would like to work.

Additional Information

International Brotherhood of Electrical Workers
900 Seventh Street NW
Washington, DC 20001
http://www.ibew.org

Junior Engineering Technical Society
1420 King Street, Suite 405
Alexandria, Virginia 22314
http://www.jets.org

National Association of Power Engineers
One Springfield Street
Chicopee, Massachusetts 01013
http://www.powerengineers.com

Related Web Sites

Electric Power Supply Association
http://www.epsa.org
Viewers of this Web site can access news articles about the energy and utility industry.

eWEEK.com
http://www.eweek.com
This resource features engineering news and links to related Web sites.

Power Plant
http://www.powerplant.com
This Web site provides links to information and articles about electricity, petroleum, nuclear energy, renewable energy, electric power engineering, and utilities.

Powering a Generation of Change: A Look Back
http://www.americanhistory.si.edu/powering
Viewers can find articles about the history of electric power and its generation at this Web site.

Testing Your Interests

How can you know if you are suited to this occupation? Ask yourself these questions. If you answer "yes" to most of them and the job sounds interesting, you may want to look into this vocation further as a possible career.

1. Am I interested in and do I have an aptitude for science and mathematics?

2. Do I enjoy analyzing problems and developing solutions?

3. Do I enjoy learning about how things work?

4. Am I persistent and thorough in my work?

5. Am I interested in power sources and utility distribution?

Published by Finney Company, Minneapolis, Minnesota 55426-4505
© Finney Company 2005

Occupational Guidance

Modeling Instructor

Description of Work

Modeling Instructors teach individuals the skills necessary to be models. Most of these professionals were previously or are currently models. In addition to utilizing written materials and resources, they may incorporate their own experiences and tips into their lessons.

Many schools offer course work for students ranging from adult women and men to teenagers to preteens. Individuals may attend modeling classes for reasons other than learning to become a model. For example, some students want to develop self-confidence, while other individuals want to learn to present a positive image in business or social situations. Instructors need to adapt the courses to meet the expectations and needs of each student.

Some Modeling Instructors specialize in certain areas of class work, while other professionals teach a wide range of courses. The programs schools offer typically include from ten to twenty weeks of classes. Each class generally lasts from two to four hours. During a class, students may learn about several topics. For example, a specialist may introduce the students to skin care and makeup, starting with personal analyses of the individuals' facial structure and skin color. This professional may also teach students about shaping their eyebrows and using cleansers and cosmetics. An expert in nutrition may offer instruction about diet guidelines and the nutritional values of the basic food groups. A certified exercise instructor may present a session on stretching, body toning, movement, and dance. Students also typically learn about hair care and styling during at least one class.

Modeling Instructors usually try to prepare students to handle a variety of assignments and situations. Prospective runway models need to learn to move their hips and shoulders in ways that draw attention to the clothing they are wearing. Students who are training for a beauty pageant should learn to carry their body in a different posture than that of runway models. Pageant contestants should be poised, keep their chin up, and use their hands in monitored movements. Prospective print advertising models need to be able to flex their body in lithe motions or hold a pose for minutes

at a time. When they lead a class on modeling on a runway, instructors usually have the students practice in front of hot lights. Individuals learn how to walk and turn on the runway and how to use props. Modeling Instructors observe the students' styles and movements and offer suggestions for improvement.

In classes that focus on fashion, teachers analyze students' wardrobes. They may offer advice about the colors and styles that flatter each student and recommend changes.

Many working models are also actors in television commercials or film. To prepare individuals for this aspect of the career, instructors may teach students about basic acting techniques. Some of these professionals also focus on the basics of speech and the use of voice in their classes. They may help students work with photographers and begin building professional portfolios. In addition, individuals in modeling programs may learn how to find agencies to represent them, how to conduct themselves during interviews, and how to prepare for auditions.

Modeling Instructors need to know how to help an attractive person look distinctively beautiful and meet modeling standards. In the past, many models presented a perfect appearance in which every hair was in place. The present-day trend for models requires individuals to appear more natural than in the past and project a dramatic, spontaneous, or waif-like image. They typically apply makeup so it appears natural and is less noticeable than the makeup styles of past models. Modeling standards generally continue to require individuals to have good skin, straight teeth, full lips, good facial bone structure, a slim and well-proportioned body, and luxuriant hair, however. Individuals may also need to be within a certain height range to work in this field.

Despite specific modeling standards, many agencies search for models who have a distinctive flair. For example, Lauren Hutton, who became famous as a model, is known for her unique face. Her nose is slightly bent, her chin points slightly to one side, and she has a cast in one eye that makes her eye seem a bit crossed. She has a gap between her two front teeth, and her lips tip up on the right and down on the left. These features add to her distinctive beauty. Modeling

GOE 01.08.01/O*Net 31317

O*Net-Soc 25-3021.00

Instructors try to help each prospective model achieve an individual look.

Individuals who are interested in this career may also want to read about related occupations, including Fashion Model (*Occupational Guidance* Vol. I, Unit 3H, No. 15), Cosmetologist (Vol. II, Unit 1I, No.15), Cosmetics Demonstrator (Vol. II, Unit 4H, No. 4), Actor (Vol. II, Unit 2I, No. 8), and Fashion Coordinator (Vol. V, Unit 5H, No. 9).

Earnings

Most individuals in this profession work part-time as instructors. They may have additional careers as cosmetologists, media experts, hair stylists, or acting coaches. Modeling Instructors usually earn around $25 an hour, depending on their level of experience and the location and reputation of the modeling school. Some individuals who are experts in specialty areas earn $40 or more an hour. In general, instructors earn from about $20,000 to $49,000 per year.

Full-time employees typically receive benefits, including paid holidays and vacation time, sick leave, and health insurance. Many professionals in this field are part-time employees, however. Employers do not usually offer these individuals benefits in addition to their wages.

History of Occupation

In the 1600s, people in Paris displayed fashions on *mannequins*, which were wooden dolls. In the 1830s, fashion professionals in England started to use drawings of models. These drawings were published in *Godey's Lady's Book*. The magazine promoted sophisticated clothing and fashions that people would then hire dressmakers to sew for them.

Charles Frederick Worth was a European dress designer in the 1850s. He asked his wife, Marie Vernet, to model his clothing. She became the first live model. With Marie Vernet's help, Frederick Worth changed the trade of dressmaking into an art form. He inspired fashion trends that spread across Europe.

After photography was invented, the fashion industry started to use this technology to produce mass-printed fashion spreads and feature articles that showcased live models. By the 1920s, movie stars were wearing designer garments to promote fashion houses. Around this time, John Robert Powers started the first modeling agency. With the invention of television, models like Candy Jones and Suzy Parker became celebrities. In the 1960s, England's Twiggy and Naomi Sims, who was the first famous African-American female model, also became celebrities. Cheryl Tiegs and Christie Brinkley were some of the most famous American models in the 1970s.

In the 1980s, agencies and advertisers began to increase the variety of models they hired. People of various ethnic backgrounds and ages modeled different sizes and styles of clothing. The trends of men's modeling changed. The fashion industry started to photograph men in seductive and intellectual poses, rather than emphasizing a traditionally rugged appearance. The modeling field has continued to change. Modeling Instructors need to stay knowledgeable about trends in the field and help their students meet the fashion standards, while achieving an individual look.

Working Conditions

Most modeling schools are comfortable and decorated in a stylish fashion. They are typically clean and well-equipped environments. Schools may have rooms set up with a runway, video recording equipment, makeup tables, and hair styling equipment. Teachers usually try to create a friendly and supportive atmosphere in order to encourage students. Classes are often small. Instructors may teach from five to fifteen students in each course.

Modeling Instructors may occasionally need to travel to organize programs in different areas. Many instructors also spend time speaking to social or professional groups or presenting seminars on makeup or fashion. These individuals may travel with a group of students to a fashion show. In addition to teaching, some of these professionals are involved in related work, such as modeling or acting.

Hours of Work

Each school's schedule may vary, but these institutions typically maintain both day and evening hours for their students. Most individuals in this profession work part-time as instructors. They may teach from two- to four-hour sessions one or more times a week. A few instructors work full-time. Schools may schedule classes during day, evening, or weekend hours, in order to meet the needs of their students.

Ability Required

Modeling Instructors often serve as role models for their students. These professionals need to dress appropriately and present a neat and fit appearance. They should have strong communication skills and be able to work with people of varying ages and backgrounds.

Temperament Required

Instructors need to be willing to help other people achieve a distinctive look and be successful, despite the teachers' personal career ambitions. They should be poised and present a confident, charming, and enthusiastic demeanor when interacting with others. Instructors should also be tactful, patient, and supportive in order to help students build self-esteem and develop modeling skills.

Education and Training Required

Individuals who are interested in this career may attend a career and technical institute to learn modeling skills. Many schools require candidates for an instructor position to be licensed to teach postsecondary education. The regulations for licensure typically differ from state to state. Some

Modeling Instructors have a college degree in an area such as nutrition, physical education, fashion design and merchandising, psychology, fine or performing arts, or other related fields. Other teachers are licensed cosmetologists or have a background in dance, acting, modeling, or business. Many schools that prepare people for a modeling career require teachers to have at least 3 years or 600 hours of modeling experience. When they secure a position, these individuals usually complete a training and orientation program at the employing school. During this training, they may observe other teachers' classes, study the school's curriculum, and be monitored by a supervisor during their first few presentations.

Finances Required Before Earning

Individuals who pursue a cosmetology degree at a career and technical school usually pay from $2,000 to $7,000 for tuition at public institutions, or from $4,000 to $15,000 for tuition at private schools. Students of modeling schools may pay from $750 to $1,500 for ten to twenty weeks of course work. At a public four-year college or university, tuition often costs between $6,000 and $16,000 a year. Students from out of state may pay additional fees. Tuition at private colleges can cost from $15,000 to more than $30,000 a year. Students should also budget for living expenses, which frequently range from $5,000 to $15,000 a year. Books and supplies may cost about $1,000 each year.

Financial Aid Information

For a free booklet on financial aid, one may write to or e-mail the following:
Financial Aids for Students
Finney Company
3943 Meadowbrook Road
Minneapolis, Minnesota 55426-4505
feedback@finney-hobar.com

Attractive Features

Many people in this profession enjoy the glamorous atmosphere of the fashion industry. Instructors may feel a sense of accomplishment or satisfaction when their students build confidence, learn new skills, and improve their appearance and poise. Teachers have opportunities to interact directly with a variety of people. Most schools provide comfortable work spaces for these professionals.

Disadvantages

Modeling Instructors often conduct classes at times that are convenient for their students, so they may need to work some evening and weekend hours. Some people dislike this schedule because they feel it interferes with their personal life. In addition to advising others about their appearance, teachers need to be well dressed and well groomed when they interact with their students and other professionals in this field. These individuals may need to spend considerable amounts of time caring for their hair, skin, and clothing to achieve this appearance.

Outlook for the Future

Candidates for a position as a Modeling Instructor will likely face strong competition. Applicants with a college degree who have been successful in the fashion or modeling industry and who have some teaching experience will probably have an advantage over other candidates in securing a position in this field. Experts predict that the fastest growing segment of modeling instruction will likely involve teaching girls in the thirteen- to fourteen-year-old bracket. Therefore, individuals who have experience working with people in this age range should also have an advantage over other candidates in obtaining a teaching position. Applicants may find employment opportunities as current instructors transfer to other occupations or retire from the workforce.

Licensing, Unions, Organizations

In the United States, a state's department of education typically issues teaching certificates for career and technical school instructors. Individuals who are working as models may be able to join a union, such as the Screen Actors Guild or the American Federation of Television and Radio Artists. These organizations offer membership to candidates who have appeared in at least one television or radio commercial. Unions often provide information about employment opportunities to their members.

Suggested Courses in High School

Individuals who are interested in this career can develop their communication skills through high school English and speech classes. Through art and family and consumer sciences courses, students can gain basic knowledge of fashion, style, color, and nutrition. Individuals who enroll in performing arts classes can develop poise and confidence. Students who plan to attend a college or university should also take college-preparatory classes, including courses in mathematics, social studies, science, and a foreign language.

Suggested High School Activities

Students can gain experience speaking and performing in front of groups of people through activities like a school drama club, debating society, or student government group. Individuals can also gain confidence by participating in these and other extracurricular activities.

Methods to Enter Work

Candidates for an instructor position can contact modeling schools for which they would like to work to learn about employment opportunities and qualification requirements. Most modeling opportunities and schools are located in cities in which advertisers conduct advertising shoots. National magazine advertisements and television commercials, followed by catalog advertisements and designer collections, provide the largest number of employment opportunities for models.

In the United States, most advertising dollars are spent in New York City. As a result, the city serves as a center for models, advertising agencies, photographers, and fashion houses. Chicago is a center for catalog companies, catalog models, and some fashion conventions. There are also many fashion shows in Dallas, which is known for its apparel market. Los Angeles and Hollywood typically have the largest number of film and television acting opportunities. Advertisers in Detroit make most print and television commercials for automobiles. In San Francisco, models typically work in the areas of print advertisements and fashion shows. In addition, many other cities in the United States have modeling schools, fashion shows, and employment opportunities for models.

Additional Information

Accrediting Commission of Career Schools and Colleges of Technology
2101 Wilson Boulevard, Suite 302
Arlington, Virginia 22201
http://www.accsct.org

Related Web Sites

Daily Fashion Report
http://www.lookonline.com/blogger.html
Viewers can find articles, editorials, book reviews, and interviews relating to the fashion industry at this Web site. Individuals can also access schedules of fashion show events and model profiles.

Fashion-411
http://www.fashion-411.com
This resource features information about fashion trends, news, shopping guides, current collections, and links to fashion designer Web sites.

Modelresource.com
http://www.modelresource.com
This Web site provides industry news, information about agencies and modeling schools, career tips, and a glossary of modeling industry terms.

Model News
http://www.modelnews.com/index.cfm
Viewers of this Web site can find modeling news, tips about modeling and ways to improve physical appearances, information about modeling scams, related Web sites, and other information.

Testing Your Interests

How can you know if you are suited to this occupation? Ask yourself these questions. If you answer "yes" to most of them and the job sounds interesting, you may want to look into this vocation further as a possible career.

1. Am I willing to maintain a healthy diet and exercise routine to stay physically fit throughout my career?

2. Am I willing to spend the necessary amounts of time and money caring for my skin and hair and updating my wardrobe?

3. Am I interested in fashion?

4. Am I interested in teaching other people?

5. Am I confident and self-disciplined?

Published by Finney Company, Minneapolis, Minnesota 55426-4505
© Finney Company 2005

Occupational Guidance

Store Designer

Description of Work

Store Designers serve as creative planners for different types of businesses and brands. They work with the businesses' executives to develop attractive and profitable shops and stores. These professionals typically have a background in architecture, visual merchandising, or interior design.

When a business owner plans to invest in a new store or expand a current facility, this individual may consult several professionals, including a city planner, an advertising executive, an architect, and a Store Designer, for advice about the best way to make the investment profitable. Planning experts often review research regarding consumer habits when advising business owners. They may use this research as an aid in making decisions about the best location, size, architecture, use, lighting, and decor for a store.

When they start their portion of the planning process, Store Designers consider many different aspects of a client's business, including the physical facilities, the inner operations, the flow of employees and customers, methods to display merchandise, the probable volume of business, and ways to make the interior of the store aesthetically pleasing. They typically plan a store's layout from the front display window to the stock areas in the rear of the facility. These professionals' primary goal in designing a facility is to help the business generate revenue.

Designers meet with the owner or operator of the facility to gather information about the geographical area surrounding the business, the employment backgrounds and the levels of disposable income of the clientele, and the owner's financial objectives for the business. With this information, they can determine how many square feet the facility needs to have, how much inventory storage they should anticipate, and what type of general decor they should select. These professionals may also be able to identify the amount of space, the type of display areas, and the appropriate type of lighting for specific departments.

Designers typically ask the store's owner about the amount of money the individual has budgeted for the layout, the type of merchandise the store plans to sell, the kinds of customers who buy the merchandise, and the number of employees who will work in the store. They then compare this information to the physical layout of the store. If they are planning a design for a facility that currently exists, they may not be able to alter much of the store's layout. If they are working with a facility that is in the process of being built or is under construction, however, these professionals may contact the architect and request that the builders include certain details in the construction of the facility. For example, a designer may request a certain kind and size of front display window.

Store Designers are generally responsible for handling all the details involved in the interior decor of an establishment. They frequently use computer-aided design (CAD) technology to create and visualize a final layout. They need to arrange merchandise display areas efficiently and appealingly while designing the spaces in accordance with federal, state, and local laws, including building codes and accessibility standards for people who are disabled or elderly. Working with the store owner, they make decisions regarding the color scheme, the furniture, the number and locations of display cases, the storage space for employees' clothing, the facility's restrooms, the space for office work, the floor coverings, and the stockroom. Designers plan a store to complement the merchandise it will sell. For example, they probably would not design a wedding boutique to resemble a hardware store.

When they submit the finished plans, these professionals typically include CAD drawings to scale, sketches, and cost estimates. After they obtain the store owner's or manager's approval of the plans, designers order the materials they need to complete the job. They select or design patterns and fabrics for draperies and furniture and choose a drapery maker and an upholsterer according to the individuals' quality of work and the prices they charge. Designers may also buy furnishings at a factory and have them delivered in time to set up the furnishings in the store before it opens. These professionals may hire plumbers, painters, carpenters, and

GOE 01.02.03/O*Net 34044
O*Net-Soc 27-1026.00

other specialists to complete different jobs. They then serve as supervisors and make sure the work is done satisfactorily.

On a typical workday, a Store Designer may attend conferences with clients to discuss the progress of projects and visit vendors that sell materials such as light fixtures, carpeting, upholstery, drapery fabrics, and display cabinets. This professional may stop at a future store's location to check the progress of the job. The individual may then spend time completing drawings for a new store or revising plans to comply with a client's suggestions. If the designer needs ideas or inspiration, the individual may visit other commercial and public facilities, such as restaurants, retail shops, or art museums. This professional may also spend some time studying the needs of a new client or doing research online or at a library.

Store Designers who work for large companies that have numerous stores may specialize in one phase of design work, such as choosing or creating display cases, rather than handling all the phases of the stores' designs. These specialists may have some variety in their work, however. For example, they may have opportunities to design display cases for different types of retail environments, such as a jewelry department and a pharmacy.

Individuals who are interested in a profession that requires similar artistic abilities and design skills may also want to read about the careers of Visual Merchandiser (*Occupational Guidance* Vol. III, Unit 4H, No. 11), Interior Designer (Vol. IV, Unit 1I, No. 16), Set Designer (Vol. II, Unit 4H, No. 7), Architect (Vol. IV, Unit 5H, No. 17), and Architectural Drafter (Vol. II, Unit 1I, No. 13).

Earnings

Store Designers' incomes vary according to their level of experience and talent and whether they are self-employed or work for a design company. Employees of design companies who have one or two years' experience may earn from $29,000 to $39,000 a year. Designers who have extensive experience can earn from $45,000 to more than $90,000 a year.

Self-employed Store Designers' motivation, skill, and ability to obtain clients affect their income. Some self-employed individuals work part-time and concentrate on a few small jobs. Other designers work full-time. They may design stores for large retail businesses or for many small shops.

Full-time employees may receive benefits in addition to their salaries. Employers often provide health insurance; paid sick leave, vacation time, and holidays; and a retirement plan. Self-employed designers need to pay for their own benefits.

History of Occupation

In the 1950s, the number of shopping centers in suburban areas in the United States started to grow. As a result, many store owners began to hire people to design their facilities.

Store Designers helped new stores attract customers. They also helped established businesses expand and remodel their current facilities.

Store Designers continue to help retail establishments decide how to display products and attract potential buyers. They provide practical plans for traffic control and flow as well as efficient storage of stock. Every year, consumers' choices of merchandise expand. In order to help businesses stay competitive, designers may do research and review studies that indicate what consumers find appealing and what influences them to make a purchase.

Working Conditions

Store Designers usually have well-designed and comfortable office spaces, because they advertise their skills to potential customers through the design of their own business establishment. These professionals frequently meet with clients at their office, so they usually have conference space and access to the equipment they need to create store layouts.

Designers also work with general contractors and store-fixture manufacturers. They spend some time shopping for suitable accessories and furnishings. As a result, these individuals may do a considerable amount of driving throughout the course of a workday. They may handle jobs in many different places. Their working conditions at these locations change from site to site. For example, an upholsterer's shop may be cluttered, and a store that is not yet finished may smell of fresh paint.

Hours of Work

Store Designers generally work during regular business hours, from about 8:00 am to about 5:00 pm, Monday through Friday. They may sometimes schedule appointments during the evening for a client's convenience, however. Designers typically work at least forty hours a week and may often work overtime in order to meet with clients and complete store plans. Many individuals in this profession work as freelancers. They have the freedom to set their own schedule.

Ability Required

Store Designers need to be able to multitask and handle many details at once in order to complete their work by set deadlines. They need to have good physical and mental stamina to handle the variety of activities they complete and the stress of their work. These professionals should be able to take a fresh approach to each project. They need to have excellent communication skills in order to explain plans to clients and describe what they want to accomplish. Store Designers need to be able to gain the confidence of potential clients. They should have artistic ability in order to prepare plans and sketches for clients. These individuals should also have a good sense of color, detail, balance, and proportion. They need to be able to use design software, including computer-aided design (CAD) programs.

Temperament Required

Designers should be creative and detail-oriented. They should make a good impression when meeting potential clients. They need to be capable and reliable individuals. These professionals should enjoy working with people and be tactful and patient in their interactions with others. They should be comfortable making decisions and confident in making suggestions. Designers should be willing to work with clients and other professionals to develop a satisfactory plan. They need to work well under pressure.

Education and Training Required

Individuals who have completed two to three years of education at a career and technical school and who have some experience in related fields may qualify for a position as a Store Designer. Most employers prefer to hire candidates for a position in this field who have a bachelor's degree in interior design or architecture in addition to practical experience, however. Regardless of the type of degree they have, individuals typically work in an entry-level position when they first enter this field. Most employers provide from four to six weeks of full-time, on-the-job training for new employees.

Some design associations suggest that prospective Store Designers take courses in interior design, graphics and color, structural design, the history of art, English, a foreign language, furniture design, the mechanical equipment of buildings, experimental design, the presentation of merchandise, sociology, psychology, and history or science while they obtain a bachelor's degree. Through social science courses, students can learn about the psychology of buying and how customers react to their immediate environments. Individuals who want to enter this career may also benefit from taking courses in architecture and computer-aided design (CAD).

Finances Required Before Earning

Prospective Store Designers should plan to pursue post-secondary education. At public career and technical schools and community colleges, tuition can cost from $2,000 to $7,000 annually. Private career and technical schools may charge from $4,000 to $15,000 each year for tuition. Public home-state universities may charge from $6,000 to $16,000 annually for tuition. Students from out of state often pay additional fees. At private colleges, tuition may cost from $15,000 to more than $30,000 a year. Students should also budget for living expenses, which frequently range from $5,000 to $15,000 per year. Books and supplies may cost about $1,000 per year.

Financial Aid information

For a free booklet on financial aid, one may write to or e-mail the following:

Financial Aids for Students
Finney Company
3943 Meadowbrook Road
Minneapolis, Minnesota 55426-4505
feedback@finney-hobar.com

Attractive Features

Many Store Designers appreciate the variety of tasks involved in their work and the opportunities that they have to be creative. They may also appreciate the unique challenge each project presents. These professionals have opportunities to be part of the progress of a project from its beginning to its end. They may gain a sense of accomplishment and satisfaction when they see the completed store.

Disadvantages

Some people dislike the level of detail work involved in this career and how busy their schedules can be at times. Store designers work under the pressure of deadlines, which many individuals find stressful. They may frequently be interrupted with problems or issues they need to handle while they are trying to finish another task. Some people find these interruptions to be irritating. Individuals who dislike interacting with many different people on a daily basis may not be suited for this career.

Outlook for the Future

As the population in the United States increases and the commercial construction industry grows, there will likely continue to be a strong employment market for Store Designers. Candidates will probably face a great deal of competition for available jobs, however, since many people enter this profession each year. People who have a bachelor's degree in an accredited design program and some architectural training may have an advantage over other applicants in securing an entry-level position in this field. Individuals who have some retail or commercial design experience and who stay informed about new technological systems and their uses should also have a competitive advantage in the job market.

Licensing, Unions, Organizations

Some states in the United States require Store Designers to be licensed. In addition, these individuals can join the Institute of Store Planners if they meet the professional organization's experience and training requirements. Some design specialists also join the American Society of Interior Designers, Inc. These two groups promote the work of interior designers, professional store planners, and people in related fields. Employers and store owners who want to hire designers often consider membership in a professional association to be a mark of achievement. In order to qualify for membership in a professional organization, individuals usually need to complete three or four years of advanced education in design and have at least two years of practical experience in the field. They then need to pass an examination administered by the National Council for Interior Design.

Suggested Courses in High School

Students who are interested in this field should take college-preparatory courses, including classes in English, mathematics, science, social studies, and a foreign language. They can also benefit from taking as many art courses as possible. Through computer and computer-aided design (CAD) courses, industrial technology classes, and courses in psychology and history, students can gain background knowledge for their future work in this career.

Suggested High School Activities

By participating in extracurricular activities such as the debate or speech team, individuals who are interested in this career can improve their communication skills. Students may be able to develop their artistic and creative skills by joining an art club and working with stage sets for school plays. They can study store designs by visiting different facilities and observing their visual marketing techniques. Prospective Store Designers can gain applicable experience for this career by working part-time or during the summer in a retail store.

Methods to Enter Work

Entry-level candidates for a position in this field may be able to gain applicable experience by working in a closely related occupation. For example, they may be able to obtain a position as a sales associate or display setter in a large department store. Employers may advertise available positions through the classified sections of newspapers and through state and private employment agencies. In addition, candidates can apply directly to companies in the store design field for which they would like to work.

Additional Information

American Society of Interior Designers, Inc.
608 Massachusetts Avenue NE
Washington, DC 20002-6006
http://www.asid.org

Foundation for Interior Design Education Research
146 Monroe Center NW, Suite 1318
Grand Rapids, Michigan 49503-2822
http://www.fider.org

National Association of Schools of Art and Design
11250 Roger Bacon Drive, Suite 21
Reston, Virginia 20190
http://nasad.arts-accredit.org

Related Web Sites

ddi **Magazine**
http://www.ddimagazine.com/displayanddesignideas/index.jsp
Viewers of this Web site can find information about major retailers and their store designs and visual presentations. They can also access a design center, a buyer's guide, a profit guide, reports and analysis, business resources, and information about industry events.

Retail Traffic **Magazine**
http://retailtrafficmag.com
This Web site features information about real estate, retail, and development and offers a section that focuses specifically on retail design.

Testing Your Interests

How can you know if you are suited to this occupation? Ask yourself these questions. If you answer "yes" to most of them and the job sounds interesting, you may want to look into this vocation further as a possible career.

1. Do I like to plan, create, and arrange the interiors of rooms and facilities?
2. Do I enjoy working with a variety of people on a daily basis?
3. Am I patient and tactful in my interactions with others?
4. Am I detail-oriented in my work and able to focus on multiple tasks at one time?
5. Do I handle stress and the pressure of deadlines well?

Published by Finney Company, Minneapolis, Minnesota 55426-4505

Occupational Guidance

Driver Training Instructor

Description of Work

Each day millions of people throughout the United States drive automobiles to go to work, school, or various other locations. Many states require individuals who are under the age of eighteen to complete driver training courses and at least six hours of behind-the-wheel training before they can apply for a driver's license. High schools frequently offer driver education courses. Some school systems require students to take such courses.

Driver Training Instructors may teach high school students and adults to drive a vehicle. Many individuals in this profession are high school teachers. They may offer instruction for high school students on weekdays and conduct adult classes in the evenings or on weekends. Commercial driver training schools and some organizations affiliated with local chapters of automobile clubs also employ Driver Training Instructors.

Teachers in this field typically start a training program with a minimum of thirty hours of classroom instruction. They introduce students to the rules of the road, good driving attitudes, the general mechanical details of automobiles, drivers' financial responsibilities, and other information. During classroom instruction, these professionals try to prepare students for the driving permit examination. Individuals who pass the examination obtain a permit, which is a preliminary license that most states require. With this permit, they can drive a car when a qualified instructor or licensed adult driver is in the vehicle. Students who have a permit can begin the behind-the-wheel portion of training.

Training programs typically provide a vehicle for students to operate during the practical portion of their training. Many of these vehicles have a second set of pedals located near the instructor's feet, so the Driver Training Instructor has some control over the automobile. In the past, some training vehicles had dual steering wheel mechanisms, but few programs continue to use these devices. The dual steering wheels often presented more of a hazard than a safety measure if both the student and the instructor tried to steer the car at the same time.

Many training programs for adults do not include classroom instruction. Instead, these programs focus primarily on the practical portion of training. Most people can learn to adequately control an automobile after fifteen to twenty hours of practical instruction.

Some high school programs have a classroom simulator or a driving range. Students practice driving in this environment during the initial portion of behind-the-wheel training. In the first hour, they may practice starting the automobile, backing up, and parking the vehicle in a large parking lot. Instructors observe how the student reacts behind the wheel and plans future instruction accordingly. For individuals who are especially nervous, Driver Training Instructors try to offer reassurance and help them stay calm. These teachers may also provide extra explanations and tips about mechanical operations if they feel the information would help students.

In the second behind-the-wheel lesson, an instructor may begin by briefly reviewing the student's first-day experiences. This professional explains the mistakes the student needs to correct. The teacher may then direct the individual to drive out of the parking lot for the first time. During the second lesson, instructors typically have students operate the car on quiet streets or roads that have a minimum of passing or approaching vehicles. They do not often choose a completely empty street, however, in order to gradually expose students to normal traffic and maneuvers.

Driver Training Instructors typically speak only as much as necessary to direct drivers. They avoid unnecessary conversation so students can concentrate entirely on driving. During early practice sessions, teachers may observe students' eyes, posture, arm positions, and other factors that influence their driving attitude. These professionals help drivers train their eyes to watch the traffic ahead and, at the same time, scan intersections and vehicles on either side of the automobile.

Instructors typically plan the routes for students before directing them out of the parking lot. They choose routes that provide the appropriate challenges for each level of training. As students gradually gain control of the vehicle and feel comfortable behind the wheel, instructors direct these individuals to drive in increasingly heavy traffic. The students have opportunities to apply their understanding of lane control, signal for left or right turns, park, and practice other skills. Commercial driving schools typically start training students on quiet streets and move to increasingly difficult situations as the individual's driving habits and physical skills improve. Instructors usually talk students through situations and help them complete maneuvers correctly, rather than let them make mistakes.

Instructors have students practice maneuvers at a relatively slow speed, since the individuals are typically somewhat unskilled in controlling a vehicle in emergencies. If possible, these teachers may include simple emergency situations in the course. For example, an instructor may direct a student to drive onto a street that will eventually be blocked by construction barriers. The professional may also instruct the driver to operate the vehicle through a maze of one-way streets and direct the student to make left and right turns that involve lane changes. Driver Training Instructors typically use these maneuvers to test students' responses to conditions that are generally not dangerous but could be stressful for new drivers. Instructors do not tell students to perform illegal maneuvers.

While students are driving, instructors may also identify various examples of poor driving habits of the drivers in the vehicles in front of the students. For example, a teacher may explain that a driver made a lane change without signaling first or point out a car that is veering across the dividing line on a road.

Many Driver Training Instructors continually emphasize the practice of planned driving. For example, a teacher may urge a student to plan ahead one or two blocks for a future turn and determine how to best position the vehicle in order to reach the appropriate lane. Throughout the practical portion of training, instructors observe the development of students' driving reflexes and assess whether the individuals perform each act of operating a vehicle as an isolated motion or as part of the total performance.

Instructors typically teach students the fundamentals of driving in about six one-hour classes. At the end of each session, they review the day's performance and identify any skills a student especially needs to practice. Instructors may encourage students to drive their family car under the supervision of a licensed adult driver between lessons.

After the final session, teachers review and rate each student's performance and skills. Depending on the results, they may encourage the individual to apply for a state driver's license or suggest additional hours of training. Most students are ready to take the licensing test after they complete the standard course. Some states in the United States require individuals to practice driving for a certain length of time after they complete a training program before they can take the licensing examination.

People who are interested in this career may also want to read about related occupations, including Driver's License Examiner (*Occupational Guidance* Vol. IV, Unit 2I, No. 2) and Secondary School Teacher (Vol. VI, Unit 1I, No. 8). There are additional education-related careers listed in the *Occupational Guidance* Cluster Index under 11.02 Educational and Library Services.

Earnings

The incomes of Driver Training Instructors typically vary according to their level of experience and the employer for which they work. The average earnings for professionals who teach in secondary schools range from $25,000 to $44,000 per year. Instructors who work for commercial training companies typically earn about $34,000 or more annually.

Most public school teachers become members of a union. Unions negotiate benefits, including health insurance, paid sick leave or personal days, and paid holidays, for their members. Many teachers also receive retirement benefits. Commercial driving schools often provide health insurance; paid sick leave, holidays, and vacation time; and retirement benefits for full-time employees.

History of Occupation

When automobiles were first invented, drivers learned how to operate vehicles by observing others or following the seller's explanation. People started to recognize the need for professional training programs as automobiles increased in size and complexity and as the number of drivers grew. In the 1930s, some high schools in the United States established training programs to teach students how to drive. Some of these programs used mock-ups of a driver seat and dashboard with a steering wheel. Many of the programs primarily used workbooks and chalkboard instruction to teach students, however.

After World War II, states started to establish certification requirements for Driver Training Instructors. During this period, automobile clubs and commercial driving schools also started to develop instructional programs. Present-day instructors continue to work for high school programs or commercial driver training schools.

Working Conditions

Individuals in this profession typically have a comfortable work environment when they conduct the classroom portion of a program. During the practical training portion, however, they may sit for many hours in an automobile. Instructors sometimes teach students to drive in unfavorable weather conditions, but they may cancel lessons if the conditions are severe.

Hours of Work

During the school year, Driver Training Instructors who also work as secondary school teachers may conduct classes in the evenings and on Saturdays. During the summer session, they may teach the practical portion of training six or more hours a day. Employees of commercial training companies may work during regular business hours or in the evenings and on weekends, depending on the schedule set by their employer.

Ability Required

Driver Training Instructors need to be excellent and experienced drivers with an acceptable driving record. They should have good reflexes, hand-eye coordination, and hearing. These individuals also need to thoroughly understand traffic laws. They should have excellent communication skills and be able to instruct students clearly and concisely.

Temperament Required

Instructors should be patient and tolerant when interacting with students. They should enjoy working with and teaching people. These professionals should be confident, calm, and not get nervous easily.

Education and Training Required

Driver Training Instructors who are also high school teachers need to be licensed to teach by the state in which they work. They need to graduate from an accredited college and obtain a minimum of a bachelor's degree in education to qualify for a teaching license. Driver Training Instructors also need to obtain the driver education endorsements their state mandates. Individuals who are certified as a teacher's aid can conduct the behind-the-wheel portion of training, but they cannot lead classroom instruction.

Driver Training Instructors who work for commercial driver education companies also need to be certified by the state in which they work. The state department of transportation usually handles this certification. Instructors need to complete a series of training programs and tests in order to be certified. They first complete written examinations and then road examinations that test their driving and teaching abilities. Many commercial companies offer training courses to prospective driver educators.

Finances Required Before Earning

People who want to teach in a public school system need to obtain a minimum of a bachelor's degree. At public home-state universities, undergraduate tuition often costs from $6,000 to $16,000 a year. Students from out of state may pay additional fees. At private colleges, tuition can cost from $15,000 to more than $30,000 annually. Students should also budget for living expenses, which frequently range from $5,000 to $15,000 each year. Books and supplies may cost an additional $1,000 per year.

To become a Driver Training Instructor, individuals need to obtain an instructor's license. This license can cost from $50 to $100, depending on the state.

Financial Aid Information

For a free booklet on financial aid, one may write to or e-mail the following:

Financial Aids for Students
Finney Company
3943 Meadowbrook Road
Minneapolis, Minnesota 55426-4505
feedback@finney-hobar.com

Attractive Features

Many Driver Training Instructors appreciate the opportunities to interact with and teach a variety of people. They may feel a sense of satisfaction and accomplishment when they watch a student improve as a driver.

Disadvantages

Individuals in this profession face some risks of accidents when they take new drivers onto busy streets, particularly if the students are impulsive or nervous. The accident rate is not especially high in this work, however, and most accidents are minor. Instructors may find sitting for many hours in a vehicle and repeatedly directing drivers along routes to be uncomfortable and tedious at times.

Outlook for the Future

In the United States, the employment market for Driver Training Instructors will probably continue to be strong, regardless of whether individuals are public school teachers with a driver-education endorsement or employees of commercial driver-education companies. Factors such as an increasing population and growing concern about driving safety will likely contribute to the demand for instructors. In addition, the federal government may pass mandates in the future that require all public schools to offer eligible students driver-training education. Such mandates should also contribute to job growth in this field.

Licensing, Unions, Organizations

Individuals who also work as high school teachers are often members of teachers' unions. Other Driver Training Instructors do not typically join unions, however. States in the United States generally require instructors to be certified. These individuals may also need to obtain a city license. Many instructors choose to become members of the Driving School Association of the Americas or other related state organizations. Teachers in high schools can join the American Driver & Traffic Safety Education Association. Most states require instructors to renew their certifications every five years.

Suggested Courses in High School

Individuals who are interested in this career can improve their driving skills and learn about this profession by taking driver education courses. They can also benefit from taking courses in public speaking, computers, and English. In addition, prospective secondary school teachers should take college-preparatory courses, including classes in mathematics, science, social studies, and a foreign language.

Suggested High School Activities

Students who want to work as a Driver Training Instructor may be able to develop leadership and interpersonal skills by participating in various extracurricular activities. They can gain teaching experience by volunteering to tutor other students or serving as a counselor at a summer camp. These individuals may be able to practice driving by using a family vehicle. They typically need to maintain a good driving record in order to qualify for a position in this field.

Methods to Enter Work

Candidates for an instructor position with a public school system may be able to learn about employment opportunities by contacting individual school districts or the state department of education. Prospective instructors can also directly contact automobile associations or private driving schools for information about available positions and possible training opportunities. In addition, some employers advertise job openings in the classified sections of newspapers, through state or private employment agencies, or on the Internet.

Additional Information

American Driver & Traffic Safety Education Association
Highway Safety Center
Indiana University of Pennsylvania, R & P Building
Indiana, Pennsylvania 15705
http://www.adtsea.iup.edu

Driving School Association of the Americas, Inc.
6031 West Center Street
Milwaukee, Wisconsin 53210
http://www.thedsaa.org

Related Web Sites

DMV Guide
http://www.dmv.org
This nongovernment Web site provides information about each state's driving regulations and requirements. Viewers can also access information about automobile insurance, driving records, driver's education programs, vehicle history reports, and legal issues related to driving and automobiles.

U.S. Department of Transportation
http://www.dot.gov
Viewers of this Web site can access information about safety issues, transportation-related news, government regulations, and careers in the transportation industry.

Testing Your Interests

How can you know if you are suited to this occupation? Ask yourself these questions. If you answer "yes" to most of them and the job sounds interesting, you may want to look into this vocation further as a possible career.

1. Do I enjoy working with and teaching a wide variety of people?

2. Am I emotionally stable, and can I remain calm during stressful situations?

3. Am I interested in the mechanical aspects of automobiles?

4. Do I enjoy driving?

5. Can I communicate ideas and give directions clearly?

6. Do I have a good driving record?

Occupational Guidance

Residential Adviser

Description of Work

Many individuals in the United States live in group housing with other people who have common needs or circumstances. Dormitories for college students, halfway houses at which parolees live, hospice facilities that provide care for elderly people, group homes for individuals who have mental or physical disabilities, and treatment facilities for people who are chemically dependent are all examples of group living arrangements. These facilities typically have a resident leader, or Residential Adviser, who helps the group members adjust to their environment and function on a daily basis.

Residential Advisers may also be known by other titles, such as child development specialists, community living assistants, residence hall counselors, residential counselors, resident assistants, residence caregivers, or house parents. These individuals work in a variety of environments, including college dormitories, sorority and fraternity houses, penal institutions, homes for people with disabilities, boarding schools, nursing homes, rooming houses for young people, halfway houses, residential treatment facilities, and orphanages. State, county, and local governments operate some group living facilities. State or private educational institutions, private and nonprofit corporations, and religious groups may also operate these types of facilities.

The primary goal of advisers is to help residents achieve the highest level of independence. These individuals may offer direction and guidance to residents. They often apply positive modeling techniques, including redirecting residents' misguided energy, praising the individuals whenever possible, and setting a good example, rather than maintaining discipline with fear and threats. These professionals need to show residents that they are interested in and concerned about the residents' problems. In their interactions with the residents, advisers attempt to encourage intellectual, social, and cultural growth.

The duties and background requirements for individuals in this profession typically vary according to the facility and group with which they work. Some large facilities employ many advisers, each of whom specializes in handling certain duties. In contrast, small homes may only employ a few individuals, who then share the general tasks involved in the work. Some groups require constant supervision or attention, while the residents of other groups may be at work or in classes during much of the day.

The specific duties for residence hall directors at a college or university may include organizing a hall council, planning social activities, enforcing rules, and supervising students who work as resident advisers. Some schools also expect residence hall directors to serve as advisers to extracurricular student groups or help with other student activities.

Advisers in small group homes may oversee the general housekeeping duties of the residence. They may be responsible for hiring and training other employees, planning meals, ordering food and other necessary supplies, and maintaining financial records. In some facilities, advisers share these duties with a house council. This council is typically elected by or chosen from the group. In addition, individuals in this profession may complete some or all of the cleaning and cooking tasks.

People who work in residences for children with disabilities may be responsible for directing, assisting with, or completing various therapeutic or instructional duties. They may be involved in physical activities such as assisting residents with bathing and dressing, administering basic first aid, and leading outings and activities.

Some facilities do not set specific experience requirements for Residential Advisers. For example, a responsible and emotionally mature college sophomore may be able to work as an adviser, though the individual may have no prior experience in such activities. Other facilities prefer to employ people who have many years of experience as advisers. In addition, some residences employ a married couple to serve as joint Residential Advisers. In such circumstances, the couple may share the duties, though one of

GOE 10.01.02/O*Net 27307
O*Net-Soc 39-9041.00

these individuals may have additional employment outside of the residence facility.

Residential Advisers continuously need to remain aware of the objectives that have been established for the group. These objectives may vary according to the ages of the residents, the reasons the residents are living in the facility, and other special circumstances or considerations. For example, a sorority adviser may spend many hours planning and chaperoning social functions. In contrast, a child development supervisor may devote much of the workday to keeping children with emotional disturbances from harming themselves or others.

Regardless of the specific setting in which they work, individuals in this profession typically attempt to understand the physical, psychological, and emotional needs of the residents. They also need to understand the regulations that affect the group and the facility's operation, since advisers are generally responsible for enforcing the rules of the residence facility.

Individuals who are interested in this career may also want to read about related occupations, including Social Worker (*Occupational Guidance* Vol. IV, Unit 1I, No. 2), Child-Care Provider (Vol. VI, Unit 1I, No. 9), and Housekeeper-Companion (Vol. VIII, Unit 2I, No. 15). Additional careers related to this profession are listed in the *Occupational Guidance* Cluster Index under the classification Humanitarian (10).

Earnings

Residential Advisers' earnings typically vary according to the type and size of their employer. The average annual salary for individuals in this profession is about $21,000. Most advisers earn between $18,000 and $27,000 a year. The lowest-paid individuals earn about $13,000 annually, while the highest-paid advisers earn about $30,000 a year.

Employers may offer benefits to individuals in this profession in addition to their salary. Some advisers receive room or board, or both. Individuals who work at a university may be able to take classes at a reduced tuition rate. Some employers also provide medical insurance and paid sick leave, holidays, and vacation time.

History of Occupation

In the 20th century, many of the living conditions and regulations of group facilities and institutions changed. For example, there were many orphanages in the United States in the past, but few such facilities currently exist. Instead, children who would previously have lived in orphanages are placed into the care of foster families or live in houselike residences with other children in need of care.

Many of the orphanages of the past were structured like military barracks. They had rows of beds in dormitories and large cafeterias with long tables. Present-day group homes for children are typically organized under the cottage system, in which relatively small groups of children live under the care and supervision of a house parent or married couple. This system of care is more expensive than the previous system of barrack-like orphanages, but the proportion of children who can successfully transition into a more traditional form of family life has increased.

Group homes for adults with special needs also try to promote reintegration with society, rather than serving as a permanent home as many institutions had in the past. These facilities try to help individuals develop the skills they need to eventually live on their own without assistance.

There have been changes in the penal system, as well, with the development of halfway houses. Many juveniles and adults who have been released from a correctional institution need time to readjust to society. These individuals often live at a halfway house for a specific period of time before they reenter society.

In addition, many schools and colleges have adjusted the regulations and living conditions of student dormitories. Rather than presenting a stiff and regimented living arrangement, most present-day dormitories try to create a homelike atmosphere for students. The previous goal of Residential Advisers in these facilities was typically to enforce strict rules promoting specific behaviors and habits. While they still enforce the facility's regulations, these individuals are also concerned about helping individuals adjust to college life and take advantage of the available opportunities.

Working Conditions

Individuals who work in a university dormitory, boarding school dormitory, or group home often have access to clean and well-furnished living quarters, adequate privacy, and full meals. In contrast, advisers in other facilities may work in a crowded institutional environment due to a lack of funds. Some individuals in this profession are continuously busy, while other advisers have slow periods during the day when the residents are at work or attending classes. Regardless of their specific schedules, Residential Advisers generally need to be available to handle emergency situations at any time of the day or night.

Hours of Work

Residential Advisers who work with boarding school or college students may have a loosely organized schedule. They may be busy some days and occasionally have days during which they only work a few hours. These individuals can often take off the time they need or want for vacations or other personal reasons. They may have their summers free for their own recreation or to work in other positions. Despite the flexibility of their schedule at times, these advisers need to remain available to guide and listen to residents.

In facilities that follow a regimental schedule, advisers may work a standard shift and have certain days off each week. Some of these individuals regularly work about forty hours a week. If an emergency situation arises, however, they may need to work overtime.

Ability Required

Residential Advisers need to have excellent interpersonal and communication skills in order to effectively establish relationships with residents while enforcing rules or treatment plans. They should have good judgment and be able to make decisions quickly. Advisers need to understand the limits of their responsibility and authority. They may at times need to request professional medical, psychological, or other help to handle situations. These individuals should also have leadership skills. Depending on the position in which they work, they may need to have specialized technical skills, such as CPR training, as well.

Temperament Required

Advisers should present a friendly, welcoming, and open demeanor in their interactions with residents. They can benefit from having a cheerful and positive outlook. These individuals should sincerely enjoy working closely with and helping people. They need to be kind, yet they should also be firm in enforcing rules. Residential Advisers should be emotionally mature. They should remain calm during stressful situations and patient when dealing with difficult residents. Individuals in this profession should take a practical approach to solving problems. They should uphold high ethical standards and be trustworthy.

Education and Training Required

Some facilities are willing to hire candidates who have a high school diploma or the equivalent for an entry-level position in this field. Many residential facilities prefer to hire applicants who have some level of college education, however. Depending on the needs of their residents, other employers in this field require candidates to have a specific undergraduate or graduate degree. Prospective advisers who attend college may want to major in psychology, sociology, family and consumer sciences, child care, education, or nursing.

Individuals who plan to work with people who have disabilities may need to obtain special medical or therapeutic training. They may also receive on-the-job training or attend special classes that institutions organize for their advisers.

Finances Required Before Earning

Some people enter this career after obtaining their high school diploma or the equivalent. These individuals need to have enough money to pay for their living expenses until they receive their first paycheck.

Other prospective Residential Advisers choose to obtain a postsecondary degree. They should budget for the associated educational costs. At public career and technical schools and community colleges, tuition frequently costs from $2,000 to $7,000 per year. Private career and technical schools may charge from $4,000 to $15,000 annually for tuition. Individuals who attend a public home-state university typically pay between $6,000 and $16,000 a year for

tuition. Students from out of state may pay additional fees. Private colleges often charge from $15,000 to more than $30,000 per year tuition. Graduate school students may pay about the same as or slightly more than undergraduate students for tuition. Individuals should also budget for living expenses, which frequently range from $5,000 to $15,000 annually. Books and supplies may cost about $1,000 per year.

Financial Aid Information

For a free booklet on financial aid, one may write to or e-mail the following:

Financial Aids for Students
Finney Company
3943 Meadowbrook Road
Minneapolis, Minnesota 55426-4505
feedback@finney-hobar.com

Attractive Features

Residential Advisers often gain a sense of satisfaction in feeling that they are helping others through their work. They may appreciate the opportunities to work with a variety of people and see the progress the individuals make. Advisers may also appreciate the challenges and variety of tasks that accompany this career.

Disadvantages

Advisers' work can be stressful and emotionally tiring at times. In some facilities, these individuals may also find their work physically strenuous. They may feel frustrated if the residence has a lack of funds and cannot provide the resources they feel are necessary to help the residents. Some people who live on-site at a facility dislike the lack of privacy. They may also dislike constantly being in their work environment. They may find that their work schedules frequently interfere with their personal life.

Outlook for the Future

Employment experts predict that the job market for Residential Advisers will likely grow faster than the average occupation through the year 2012. Factors such as the downsizing of many institutions and the trend of bringing people with disabilities into mainstream society should have a strong impact on growth in the number of residential group homes. The number of private companies that provide residential treatment, assisted living, and independent living facilities should also increase, which in turn should lead to new employment opportunities for individuals in this profession.

Licensing, Unions, Organizations

Candidates for a position with state, county, or other government agencies may need to take a civil-service test as part of the application process. Residential Advisers often join professional organizations, such as the American Counseling Association or the American Association of Children's Residential Centers. There are other organizations that extend membership specifically to advisers in government institutions and dormitories on college campuses. In addition, some organizations promote the work of individuals who serve as advisers for people who are visually or hearing impaired, have mental or physical disabilities, or have particular illnesses.

Suggested Courses in High School

Individuals who plan to pursue postsecondary education should take college-preparatory courses, including classes in English, mathematics, science, social studies, and a foreign language. Prospective Residential Advisers can improve their communication skills by enrolling in speech classes. They may also benefit from taking courses in computers, keyboarding, family and consumer sciences, health, psychology, and physical education.

Suggested High School Activities

Students who are interested in this career can gain interpersonal and communication skills by participating in extracurricular activities such as student council, drama, debate, individual and team athletics, and art clubs. They may also develop poise, assurance, and teamwork skills through such activities. Individuals can acquire applicable experience for this career by volunteering to work with playground programs, at hospitals, at centers that treat people with disabilities, and for fund drives. They may also be able to gain experience by working at day camps, day-care centers, or nursing homes.

Methods to Enter Work

Graduates of a postsecondary institution may be able to contact their school's placement office for assistance in finding a position in this field. Private, state, or federal employment agencies may also have information about job openings for Residential Advisers. Employers may advertise available positions in the classified sections of newspapers or on the Internet. In addition, candidates can directly contact organizations for which they would like to work to inquire about employment opportunities. Applicants usually need to provide personal character references during or before the first interview.

Additional Information

American Association of Children's Residential Centers
11700 West Lake Park Drive
Milwaukee, Wisconsin 53224
http://www.aacrc-dc.org

Related Web Sites

American Counseling Association
http://www.counseling.org
This Web site provides information about counseling careers, public policy, professional conventions, and related resources.

National Board for Certified Counselors and Affiliates
http://www.nbcc.org
Viewers of this Web site can find information about certification, recertification opportunities, examinations, and ethics, in addition to other topics.

Testing Your Interests

How can you know if you are suited to this occupation? Ask yourself these questions. If you answer "yes" to most of them and the job sounds interesting, you may want to look into this vocation further as a possible career.

1. Do I enjoy working with a variety of people?

2. Do I sincerely enjoy working with and helping others?

3. Am I emotionally mature and able to handle stress well?

4. Can I remain objective in my interactions with others and in making decisions?

5. Am I able to enforce rules, regardless of whether I personally agree with them?

Published by Finney Company, Minneapolis, Minnesota 55426-4505
© Finney Company 2005

Occupational Guidance

Custom Tailor/Dressmaker

Description of Work

In the United States, most of the clothing items that consumers purchase are mass-produced, ready-to-wear garments. Some people hire Custom Tailors or Dressmakers to alter garments or create clothes specifically for them, however. Individuals may purchase custom-made clothing because they want to adapt designs or patterns to their preferences. People who wear unusual sizes or do not like the way garments in retail stores fit may also prefer to purchase custom-made dresses or suits.

Many individuals in this profession are self-employed. They may work at home or in a shop. Tailors typically make suits, coats, and jackets for men. They may also sew some suits or coats for women. Dressmakers usually specialize in women's garments, children's wear, alterations, or a combination of these specialties. Some of these professionals also perform alterations for men's clothing.

When a customer orders a garment, the Custom Tailor or Dressmaker may first help the individual select a pattern style and material. The professional sometimes goes to a customer's home or place of business, but most customers visit the sewing expert's shop. On the first visit, the professional may discuss patterns, fitting problems, the garment or garments the customer wants made, suitable materials, color, cost, and other matters with the customer. The Tailor or Dressmaker may show the customer fabric samples and offer advice about different kinds of materials or styles that would best suit the person.

The professional needs to take accurate measurements of the customer in order to fit a pattern to the individual. The Tailor or Dressmaker may use a commercial or custom-made pattern. In some cases, this individual enters measurements into a computer software program to produce a pattern. While taking the customer's body measurements, the Tailor or Dressmaker needs to note any features of the customer's figure that might make a standard size of clothing fit improperly. The individual may measure a customer's arm length, shoulder width, back seam, inseam, waist, hip size, and chest. The professional also notes the customer's

preferences, such as a specific number of buttons for a jacket or a certain width of lapels. In addition, a customer may want a vest, extra trousers, a skirt, or slacks to go with a suit.

After the professional has determined the style and fabric for the garment and taken the customer's measurements, this expert begins creating the garment. The Dressmaker or Tailor may first make a working pattern. The individual considers the nap and weave of the fabric and matches the pattern before cutting the fabric. This professional may pin or mark darts, seams, or other guidelines. The Tailor or Dressmaker needs to select proper thread for the garment and then sew the pieces together. The individual constructs the finished garment with a combination of machine and handwork. In the final steps, the Tailor or Dressmaker adds details such as buttons, buttonholes, designs, appliqué, or trim. For coats and suits, this professional may add padding, lining, interlining, and some interfacing.

The Tailor or Dressmaker may decide to arrange an intermediate fitting with a customer. Before the final fitting, the professional may brush and press the garment. The individual may then deliver the article of clothing, or the customer may come to the shop. During the fitting, the customer tries on the garment. If the customer requests slight changes, the Tailor or Dressmaker makes the necessary alterations.

Some large custom tailoring shops hire individuals who specialize in a particular area of this work. For example, the head Tailor may measure the customer and cut the fabric, another Tailor may sew the coat, and another professional may make the trousers and vest. The shop may offer made-to-measure services. If customers select such services, a professional measures the customer for the suit or other type of apparel and then sends the measurements to an off-site location where the garment is sewn. When the garment is returned to the shop, the Tailor or Dressmaker makes the final alterations.

In addition to custom-making garments, a Dressmaker or Tailor may provide alterations services for manufactured apparel. When altering a garment, the professional usually

GOE 05.05.15/O*Net 89505B
O*Net-Soc 51-6052.00

fits the article of clothing directly on the customer. The individual marks or pins the places that need changes and then asks the customer to remove the garment. To complete the alterations, the Tailor or Dressmaker may need to take apart existing seams; adjust hemlines, linings, or interfacings; or relocate zippers, snaps, or other fasteners. When the professional is finished altering the garment, the customer tries it on again to make sure it fits properly.

Some Tailors and Dressmakers work as employees of department stores or specialty shops. These individuals may make alterations on garments that customers purchase in the store. Many of these employees work full-time. Other individuals in this profession work full-time or part-time in a retail establishment and then offer tailoring, dressmaking, or alterations services from their homes. In addition, the garment and fashion industries may employ some Dressmakers. Individuals in this area of the field usually create quality or styled garments. They work directly from patterns or create apparel by draping the fabric on dress forms.

Individuals who are interested in this career may also want to read about related occupations, including Clothes Designer (*Occupational Guidance* Vol. II, Unit 1I, No. 1), Costume Designer (Vol. IV, Unit 4H, No. 18), Custom Drapery Maker (Vol. II, Unit 3H, No. 9), and Sewing Instructor (Vol. IV, Unit 5H, No. 16). They may also want to read about garment industry careers, including Patternmaker (Garment Industry) (*Occupational Guidance* Vol. VI, Unit 5H, No. 16) and Power Sewing Machine Operator (Vol. V, Unit 4H, No. 1).

Earnings

Custom Tailors' and Dressmakers' earnings typically vary according to their level of skill, their reputation, and whether they are self-employed or work for a shop or retail store. Full-time entry-level Dressmakers and Tailors in shops or clothing stores who perform alterations usually earn from about $17,000 to $20,000 a year. Employees may earn up to 50 percent of each alteration. This amount averages between $8 and $20 for each item. Experienced tailoring and dressmaking professionals employed at a shop or retail store may earn anywhere from $20,000 to $42,000 per year.

The incomes of self-employed individuals who work in the fashion industry often vary according to how many garments they create. Experienced and highly skilled professionals frequently charge from $100 to $2,000 a garment. Highly skilled Tailors who own their own business and who have a solid reputation may earn $100,000 or more each year.

Full-time employees of shops, retail establishments, or fashion design companies may receive benefits. Employers often provide health insurance, sick leave, paid holidays and vacation time, and retirement plans. Self-employed individuals typically need to pay for their own benefits.

History of Occupation

Some of the first types of clothing people made consisted of animal skins. At first, individuals draped furs over their body. People eventually started to cut the furs into shaped patterns, however. They later made needles from pieces of bone and used the needles and animal sinews to sew the furs together.

As civilizations grew, people learned to use other materials for clothing and developed different fashions. The early Egyptians used cotton, linen, and wool to make tunics and robes. The Persians cut and fit garments instead of draping them loosely. People's preferences for the styles and fabrics of clothing have changed throughout history.

For most of history, the majority of people sewed their own clothes. Wealthy or noble families could often afford to hire Custom Tailors and Dressmakers, however.

In the 18th century, the spinning machine and power loom were developed. The increased availability of cloth made it possible for many people to purchase fabric. Some of these individuals chose to hire professionals to sew garments for them.

Clothing manufacturing plants opened in the United States in the middle of the 19th century in response to the need for uniforms for the Civil War. When ready-to-wear clothing became popular, the demand for Dressmakers and Tailors declined sharply. By the 20th century, the United States was a leading country in clothing manufacturing. Some professional sewers were able to maintain small tailoring and dressmaking businesses, however.

Many present-day retail establishments hire Custom Tailors or Dressmakers to make alterations to clothing. Professionals in this field may also work for the garment and fashion industries. Some individuals maintain their own shops and create custom-made clothing for customers.

Working Conditions

Self-employed professionals can typically choose their own working conditions. They may set up their business in their home or in a shop outside of their home. These professionals work with tools like scissors, pins, and a sewing machine. Customers usually visit a Tailor's or Dressmaker's place of business, but professionals in this field may occasionally meet a customer at a location the customer chooses. When they measure customers, individuals often stoop, bend, lift, reach, and stretch.

Employees of stores or other establishments usually have adequately equipped working conditions with good lighting and temperature control. Individuals in this profession may work alone or with assistants.

Hours of Work

Self-employed professionals can set their own work hours. They usually consider the convenience of customers when setting appointments, however. They may schedule fittings in the evenings or on weekends. These individuals may be especially busy before certain holidays or when the fashion season changes. Customers often need a garment for a special occasion, such as a wedding or a vacation. Tailors and Dressmakers may sometimes need to work overtime to complete garments, while they may have few projects to complete at other times. Self-employed professionals may frequently work about sixty hours a week.

Employees of shops or other establishments typically have a regular schedule, which their employer determines. At custom tailoring shops, individuals frequently work between forty and forty-eight hours a week, usually including Saturdays.

Ability Required

Custom Tailors and Dressmakers need to have excellent sewing skills and a good sense of fashion and design. They should be knowledgeable about the procedures involved in fitting and altering garments and making patterns. These professionals should be able to visualize a finished garment as a customer describes it. In addition, they need to have good manual dexterity, good physical coordination, and excellent eyesight. Self-employed professionals should also have business and customer-service skills.

Temperament Required

Individuals in this profession should be imaginative and creative when they make garments for people who want clothing that is unusual or different from current styles. They need to be patient, good listeners, and friendly when working with others. These professionals also need to make sure their personal likes or dislikes do not affect their business relationships with customers. They should be detail-oriented, thorough, and consistent in producing high quality work.

Education and Training Required

Prospective Tailors and Dressmakers can choose from several educational paths. Some individuals take courses at a career and technical school. Through these courses, they gain practical experience in sewing, pattern-making, fashion design, and related areas. They also learn about developments in electronic and computerized equipment in this field.

Other individuals who are interested in this profession may choose to attend a four-year college or university. Many of these students major in the areas of family and consumer sciences, fashion design, or business management. They may take classes in art, color, sewing, pattern-making, and consumerism. Prospective Tailors and Dressmakers also often learn about fabric, textiles, and the history and origins of raw materials while they are in college. Some employers require candidates for a position in this field to have a bachelor's degree.

Some people enter this profession by working as assistants to experienced professionals in custom shops, retail establishments, or garment factories. As they obtain practical cutting, marking, pattern-making, and sewing experience, these individuals may have opportunities to complete increasingly complicated assignments. Regardless of their educational background, prospective Tailors or Dressmakers typically need to obtain on-the-job training.

Finances Required Before Earning

Students at public career and technical schools or community colleges may pay from $2,000 to $7,000 a year for tuition. Private career and technical schools often charge from $4,000 to $15,000 annually for tuition. The cost of tuition at public home-state universities usually ranges from $6,000 to $16,000 a year. Students from out of state may pay additional fees. Private colleges may charge from $15,000 to more than $30,000 a year for tuition. Students should also budget for living expenses, which can range from $5,000 to $15,000 annually. Books and supplies may cost an additional $1,000 per year.

Individuals who do not pursue postsecondary education and instead work as assistants need to have enough money to pay for their living expenses until they receive their first paycheck. Tailors or Dressmakers who start their own business need to purchase the necessary equipment, such as a sewing machine, scissors, thread, pattern paper, an iron, and other tools and supplies.

Financial Aid Information

For a free booklet on financial aid, one may write to or e-mail the following:

Financial Aids for Students
Finney Company
3943 Meadowbrook Road
Minneapolis, Minnesota 55426-4505
feedback@finney-hobar.com

Attractive Features

People who enjoy sewing may be interested in this career. Self-employed professionals can set their own schedules. They may appreciate the opportunities to be creative, meet different people, and complete a variety of sewing projects. Tailors and Dressmakers may feel a sense of satisfaction when they finish a garment and please a customer.

Disadvantages

Many individuals in these professions frequently work more than forty hours each week. They perform a great deal of detail work, which some people find tiring. These individuals may be at risk of eyestrain. Dressmakers and Tailors may dislike working with some customers who are impatient or dissatisfied. Professionals in this field often need to spend several years developing their reputation and business before they can earn a stable income.

Outlook for the Future

Imported garments currently make up about half of the clothing sold in the United States. As imports increase, the number of employment opportunities for Custom Tailors and Dressmakers may decrease. Individuals who offer specialty services or meet particular service needs in the apparel field may be able to establish their own business. Some people will likely continue to appreciate and prefer the quality of custom garments and alteration improvements on ready-made clothing. Tailors and Dressmakers who have strong business and customer service skills and excellent sewing skills may have an advantage over other professionals in establishing a loyal customer base.

Licensing, Unions, Organizations

Individuals do not need to be licensed to work in this field. Employees in the garment industry may choose to join a union, such as UNITE HERE. Most self-employed professionals are not union members. These individuals often join organizations, such as the American Apparel and Footwear Association, that work to advance the fashion industry, however.

Suggested Courses in High School

Students who are interested in pursuing a career as a Custom Tailor or Dressmaker should take as many sewing courses as possible in high school. Through art classes, individuals can develop an appreciation for color and design. People who hope to eventually become self-employed can benefit from enrolling in courses in mathematics, computers, and business. Some high schools also allow students to take classes at a career and technical school. Individuals who plan to attend college should take college-preparatory courses, including classes in English, history, science, and a foreign language.

Suggested High School Activities

Prospective Tailors and Dressmakers should practice sewing as much as possible. They can complete sewing projects at home or through a scouting or 4-H group. Individuals can also gain sewing experience by volunteering to create costumes for a school theater production. Students may be able to learn basic business principles by joining a business club. In addition, people who are interested in these careers can learn about the field by talking with professional Tailors or Dressmakers.

Methods to Enter Work

Many alteration shops, retail and fashion establishments, and garment factories advertise available sewing positions in the classified sections of newspapers. State or private employment agencies may have information about job opportunities for professionals in this field. Candidates can also apply directly to a shop, factory, or department store for which they would like to work.

Before individuals can start their own business, they typically need to gain experience and make contacts with prospective customers. They often advertise their services through local newspapers, by business cards, or in telephone directories.

Additional Information

American Sewing Guild
9660 Hillcroft, Suite 510
Houston, Texas 77096
http://www.asg.org

Home Sewing Association
PO Box 1312
Monroeville, Pennsylvania 15146
http://www.sewing.org

Related Web Sites

American Apparel and Footwear Association
http://www.americanapparel.org
Viewers of this Web site can find information about international trade, related publications, economic data, and industry links.

FIDM 'Zine
http://www.fidm.com/common/zinemain.html
This Web site offers fashion news and articles, information about style, and links to related resources.

Testing Your Interests

How can you know if you are suited to this occupation? Ask yourself these questions. If you answer "yes" to most of them and the job sounds interesting, you may want to look into this vocation further as a possible career.

1. Do I enjoy and have an aptitude for sewing?

2. Can I work well alone and with others?

3. Am I detail-oriented in my work?

4. Do I try to achieve a high level of quality in my work?

5. Do I have good eyesight and manual dexterity?

Occupational Guidance

Fund-Raising Director

Description of Work

Many agencies, institutions, and organizations obtain funding each year through donations from individuals, foundations, and corporations. For example, some religious organizations rely solely on donations to pay for their facilities, staff members' salaries, and other expenses. Agencies that provide public health and social welfare services often finance their programs from a combination of government funding and private donations. Colleges and universities often solicit donations from alumni and foundations to provide scholarships to students, fund educational departments, and build or renovate their buildings.

Fund-Raising Directors help organizations obtain donations. They specialize in methods of soliciting funds and are generally responsible for planning fund-raising campaigns. Many individuals in this profession work for an educational, religious, environmental, or philanthropic agency. Directors may also be known by the titles of contributions secretary, development officer, endowment vice president, and campaign leader. Regardless of their specific title, these professionals need to be thoroughly familiar with the organization for which they work. They also need to be able to identify which people, corporations, or foundations are most likely to donate to the cause and develop a reliable approach to increase contributions each year.

Directors may continually try to find new ways to solicit funds. In the past, organizations often sent a letter once a year to people they thought might donate to their cause. Although present-day organizations may continue to send letters, they often use other methods of raising money as well. For example, a Fund-Raising Director may ask an influential person, such as a community leader or a celebrity, to endorse the organization's cause and sign solicitation letters. This professional may also organize volunteers and employees or contract with a telemarketing firm to solicit funds over the telephone.

Some Fund-Raising Directors are not directly connected to the agencies or institutions for which they raise funds. Instead, they may operate as an outside consultant and have their own office or corporation. Most individuals who work as consultants have extensively studied American patterns of giving. They use their knowledge of these patterns to tailor distinctive fund-raising campaigns for their clients.

Fund-Raising Directors who work as consultants may face different challenges than directors who are members of an organization's staff. A consulting director does not typically have the same experience with a particular organization and its past campaigns as a staff director would. Outside consultants may be able to produce a more imaginative or novel campaign than a staff director would, because consultants have had exposure to other organization's methods and may be able to suggest new and non-traditional approaches. If consulting Fund-Raising Directors are successful in developing an effective campaign for an organization, the organization may become a loyal client and regularly employ the professional's services.

Regardless of whether they work as on-staff or consulting Fund-Raising Directors, these professionals have similar duties. They usually are not personally involved in efforts to solicit funds. Instead, they are primarily concerned with planning and executing a lucrative fund-raising campaign. Directors may recruit and train volunteers to handle the actual efforts to collect money.

When they develop a campaign, individuals in this profession need to consider the financial needs of the organization, whether there are sufficient numbers of volunteers available to complete the work involved in the campaign, and whether the campaign is likely to secure a sufficient amount of funds. Directors may also analyze public opinion about the agency or institution and attempt to eliminate or correct any negative factors. Once they have completed a thorough analysis, they establish the organization's need and the potential of giving.

Directors then construct the campaign. They may use a variety of fund-raising methods. For some causes, such as a college alumni contribution campaign, they may write a carefully worded letter that emphasizes the alumni's connection to the school. For others causes, directors may choose to use a grassroots plan of action. They may have

GOE 11.09.02/O*Net 13011D
O*Net-Soc 11-2031.00

volunteers make personal door-to-door requests of businesspeople and private individuals. In addition, individuals in this profession may plan events such as a charity ball, raffle, or contest to solicit funds.

Fund-Raising Directors may also be able to increase an organization's funds by submitting grant proposals to foundations, corporations, and government agencies. They typically explain the goals and needs of the organization and request grant money in these proposals. Directors may work alone on grant proposals, or they may work as a team with a professional grant writer.

Once they have established the campaign methods, Fund-Raising Directors launch the effort publicly. They or their staff members may prepare press releases and photographs. They may also directly contact radio, television, and newspaper employees to create awareness and explain details of the cause. In addition, they coordinate the volunteer solicitation phase. These professionals recruit and properly train field volunteers to collect contributions.

Directors may plan events, such as a kick-off luncheon, to coincide with the launching of the campaign. These individuals need to consider many details of each event involved in the campaign. Professionals who handle large campaigns may spend a year or more planning the different phases of the campaign.

Fund-Raising Directors need to continuously assess the progress of a campaign. They note any improvements or changes they think may increase turnout and general interest for the next year's campaign. For example, if a planned event falls close to a holiday and therefore has fewer people in attendance than may have otherwise come, these professionals may plan to schedule the event at a later or earlier time in the next year. They need to be continuously alert for new fund-raising opportunities and approaches.

Individuals who are interested in this career may also want to read about related occupations, including Public Relations Specialist (*Occupational Guidance* Vol. V, Unit 5H, No. 3), Advertising Manager (Vol. II, Unit 2I, No. 17), Alumni Relations Director (Vol. III, Unit 5H, No. 2), Grants Analyst (Foundation) (Vol. IV, Unit 2I, No. 15), and Coordinator of Volunteers (*Occupational Guidance* Vol. III, Unit 2I, No. 13).

Earnings

The earnings of Fund-Raising Directors vary according to the type of fund-raising they do and their employing institution or agency. The average income for full-time directors is about $76,000 annually. Most individuals in this profession earn between $61,000 and $94,000 per year.

Some organizations do not require a full-time Fund-Raising Director. Individuals who work for such employers often perform other functions, such as coordinating volunteers or directing public education, in addition to their fund-raising duties.

Many professionals in this field are self-employed. They work as consultants. They may base their fees on a percentage of the amount of money they need to collect, or directors may bill clients an established fee amount for the number of hours or days they spend on projects. Consultants' incomes generally vary according to the number of hours they work each week and the types of organizations for which they raise funds.

Many employers in this field provide benefits for full-time salaried employees. Directors may receive health insurance; paid vacation time, holidays, and sick leave; and retirement benefits. Self-employed consultants typically need to provide for their own health insurance and retirement savings.

History of Occupation

In the United States during World War I, the American Red Cross, the Salvation Army, and other organizations implemented new approaches to fund-raising. As a result, these groups raised significantly more money than they had in the past. After the war, some individuals who had coordinated successful fund-raising campaigns established themselves as consultants. They offered their fund-raising services to colleges, hospitals, and other agencies and institutions. In 1935, nine of the major, long-established fund-raising firms organized the American Association of Fundraising Counsel, which continues to play a role in the growth of American philanthropy.

Although people are often more reluctant to donate money during difficult economic times or a recession than during periods of economic growth, Fund-Raising Directors continued to raise money for organizations during the Great Depression of the 1930s. Millions of dollars were raised for charities through annual presidential birthday balls. The March of Dimes Birth Defects Foundation, formerly known as the National Foundation of Infantile Paralysis, also raised a significant amount of money during this period. President Franklin D. Roosevelt, who was a victim of poliomyelitis, commonly known as polio, endorsed the efforts of the March of Dimes Birth Defects Foundation.

After World War II, some fraudulent charity drives, which people had established to raise money for their own personal gain, were exposed. The ensuing publicity had a negative impact on legitimate fund drives as well.

People eventually began to regain their trust in fund-raising drives, however. Between 1940 and 1958, for example, contributions to national and local health and welfare agencies increased from $188 million to $1.5 billion. Between 1958 and 1968, contributions multiplied threefold. The donations people made to health and welfare agencies represented one-quarter of the total philanthropic giving in the United States.

According to Internal Revenue Service statistics, Americans contributed more than $20 billion to charitable causes in the early 1970s. By the early 1980s, the number of donations had again tripled, totaling more than $60 billion. By the mid-1990s, individuals were contributing more than $129 billion to charitable causes.

Many people continue to donate money to different organizations and institutions. Fund-Raising Directors play a significant role in soliciting these charitable funds. They plan and organize fund-raising drives and continually search for new ways to encourage individuals to donate to a cause.

Working Conditions

Fund-Raising Directors typically perform much of their work in a comfortable office. They often have a staff of clerical and other employees. These professionals may need to travel to different locations to prepare campaigns at various times of the year. They may frequently attend meetings in and out of the office.

Hours of Work

During a campaign, Fund-Raising Directors may work more than fifty or sixty hours a week. They may need to work evenings and weekends to handle the many details involved in organizing events. During periods when they do not have a campaign underway, however, these professionals typically work forty or fewer hours a week.

Ability Required

Individuals in this profession need to be able to sell ideas. They should have excellent verbal and written communication skills in order to give presentations, craft letters and other solicitation materials, and develop grant proposals. Directors also need to be knowledgeable about the processes involved in business administration. They should have strong project-management and organizational skills in order to coordinate effective campaigns.

Temperament Required

Fund-Raising Directors should be creative and imaginative in developing campaigns. They should be energetic and enthusiastic and have a positive attitude. Professionals in this field should work well with a variety of people and be highly diplomatic and tactful. They need to understand how to lead and inspire confidence in others. These individuals should be comfortable making and acting on decisions. They need to be emotionally stable and remain calm during stressful situations. In addition, directors should handle rejection well. Although they may feel disappointed when they do not meet monetary goals, they need to continue working on developing new strategies to solicit funds.

Education and Training Required

Many employers prefer to hire candidates for a position as a Fund-Raising Director to have a minimum of a bachelor's degree. Some employers consider a four-year degree to be a requirement for this position. Prospective directors often major in psychology, sociology, or a related field. They may also take classes in advertising, journalism, graphic arts, and public relations. Individuals can further prepare for this career by working as a junior staff member of a large charitable or nonprofit agency.

Finances Required Before Earning

Most individuals who plan to enter this career pursue a minimum of a bachelor's degree. They should budget for the associated educational expenses. At public home-state universities, undergraduate tuition often costs between $6,000 and $16,000 a year. Students from out of state may pay additional fees. Private colleges may charge from $15,000 to more than $30,000 per year for undergraduate tuition. Individuals who choose to obtain a graduate-level degree after they earn a bachelor's degree usually pay about the same as or slightly more than undergraduate students for tuition. In addition to the costs of tuition, students should budget for living expenses, which frequently range from $5,000 to $15,000 annually. Books and supplies often cost about $1,000 per year.

Financial Aid Information

For a free booklet on financial aid, one may write to or e-mail the following:

Financial Aids for Students
Finney Company
3943 Meadowbrook Road
Minneapolis, Minnesota 55426-4505
feedback@finney-hobar.com

Attractive Features

People in this career may appreciate the challenges and variety that accompany their work. They have opportunities to meet many different people and to be creative. These professionals may also appreciate their level of responsibility. They may gain a sense of satisfaction in feeling that they are helping fund the activities of charitable and nonprofit organizations.

Disadvantages

Directors may occasionally work with difficult or uncooperative people. They need to remain tactful and diplomatic during these interactions, despite their personal feelings about the individuals. Fund-raising professionals may find their work stressful at times, particularly when they need to meet deadlines. They may feel frustrated if their campaigns do not raise the necessary funds. Individuals in this profession frequently work more than forty hours a week. They may complete projects or spend time traveling in the evenings and on weekends. As a result, directors may find that their work schedule interferes with their personal life at times.

Outlook for the Future

Employment experts predict that the job market for Fund-Raising Directors will likely experience average growth through the year 2012. The rate of job growth may be slowed by government budget cuts. These cuts may result in decreased funds for nonprofit organizations, which may then need to make cuts in salaries and personnel. In addition, the number of organizations that compete for public funds is growing. Candidates for a position in this field will probably face a high level of competition. Applicants who have a college degree and strong written and verbal communication skills should have an advantage over other individuals in securing a position.

Licensing, Unions, Organizations

Many Fund-Raising Directors become members of the American Association of Fundraising Counsel. This organization provides a variety of services and published materials for directors. Individuals in this career may also join other professional organizations in related fields.

Suggested Courses in High School

Students who plan to pursue postsecondary education should take college-preparatory courses, including classes in English, science, mathematics, social studies, and a foreign language. Individuals who are interested in this career can also benefit from taking courses in keyboarding, computers, graphic arts, psychology, sociology, and journalism.

Suggested High School Activities

Prospective Fund-Raising Directors can develop leadership, teamwork, and communication skills by participating in a variety of extracurricular activities, including team athletic activities, a drama or debate club, or the student council. They can improve their writing skills by joining the staff of their school newspaper or yearbook. Individuals can gain applicable experience for this career by participating in school or community fund-raising campaigns. They can also gain experience by volunteering with charitable or nonprofit organizations.

Methods to Enter Work

Employers may advertise available positions for Fund-Raising Directors in the classified sections of newspapers, on the Internet, or through professional publications. They may also list job openings with state or private employment agencies. College graduates may be able to contact their school's placement office for assistance in finding a position. In addition, they can directly contact organizations for which they would like to work to inquire about employment opportunities. Candidates may find the names and contact information for different organizations in the business directory of their local telephone book or on the Internet.

Additional Information

American Association of Fundraising Counsel
4700 West Lake Avenue
Glenview, Illinois 60025
http://www.aafrc.org

Related Web Sites

Association of Fund-Raising Distributors & Suppliers
http://www.afrds.org
This Web site provides information about the tools fund-raising professionals use and includes links to educational resources.

Association of Fundraising Professionals
http://www.afpnet.org
Viewers of this Web site can find information about ethics, public policy, educational and career development opportunities, and related resources.

Testing Your Interests

How can you know if you are suited to this occupation? Ask yourself these questions. If you answer "yes" to most of them and the job sounds interesting, you may want to look into this vocation further as a possible career.

1. Do I enjoy working with a wide variety of people?

2. Do I enjoy planning events and activities?

3. Am I creative, imaginative, and independent in my work?

4. Am I comfortable making decisions and accepting a great deal of responsibility?

5. Do I have strong verbal and written communication skills?

Published by Finney Company, Minneapolis, Minnesota 55426-4505
© Finney Company 2005

Occupational Guidance

Judge

Description of Work

There are three branches of government in the United States: the legislative, executive, and judicial branches. The court system is part of the judicial branch. Courts determine the guilt or innocence of people accused of crimes and settle disputes between individuals. Judges serve as central figures in courtrooms.

Judges hear the evidence presented in each case. They determine whether the evidence is permissible and properly presented. For jury trials, these professionals instruct the jury of its duties. For cases that have no juries, these experts need to make a fair and impartial decision regarding each case. Individuals in this profession typically have a law degree and several years of previous experience as a lawyer.

Judges preside over civil, criminal, or appeals cases. Civil cases involve disputes, usually regarding sums of money, between individuals or corporations. In criminal cases, people who are accused of breaking laws are on trial. Appeals cases have previously been tried in a lower court, but are submitted to a higher court, called an *appellate court,* for a decision regarding legal issues with the case. Many more individuals who work in this field serve as trial Judges than appellate court Judges.

Local, state, and federal courts handle cases. The Supreme Court, which is the highest court in the United States, also hears cases. State-level courts handle most judicial actions in the United States. The lowest courts at the state level are local trial courts, also called *magistrate courts* in some states. Judges in these courts preside over minor civil or criminal cases. The penalties that individuals receive as a result of these cases do not usually exceed a fine or short-term imprisonment. There are different types of local trial courts, including traffic, police, county, small claims, juvenile, probate, and family courts. In urban areas, local trial court Judges usually work full-time. In rural areas, however, these professionals may work part-time. They may be called justices of the peace, rather than Judges. The types of cases these individuals hear do not usually require a jury.

General trial courts are the next level of state courts. General trial cases typically involve more serious criminal and civil offenses than local trial cases. At this level, cases may involve large sums of money and may result in extended terms of imprisonment for individuals who are found guilty. Each defendant in a general trial court has a right to a jury trial. Accused individuals may decide to be tried before the Judge alone, however. For such cases, the Judge hears the evidence and then issues a decision called a *judgment*. For jury trials, the jury issues a *verdict*, though the Judge usually determines and passes the sentence.

Every state in the United States has at least one appellate court. This court hears cases that have previously been tried in lower courts. Professionals who serve on the judicial bench in appellate courts review trial proceedings from the lower courts. They study written arguments, called *briefs*, which lawyers submit. Judges review the information to determine if there were errors committed during the previous trials that would justify reversing the decisions of the lower courts. They generally submit decisions regarding the court proceedings in writing and publish the decisions for reference in future court cases. Judges in subsequent trials may use these published decisions as a basis for their decisions about a trial.

The federal court system is divided into district courts. These courts also handle criminal and civil cases. Some districts may employ several Judges to handle cases. Each of these professionals works independently, however. United States courts of appeal are at a higher level than district courts. These appellate courts review the proceedings of the district courts in each area. The President of the United States is responsible for appointing federal Judges. The President also appoints the nine Judges on the United States Supreme Court. These judges hear appeals from the highest courts of the states.

Regardless of the type of court in which they work, Judges need to try to understand all aspects of each case. For criminal cases, they examine the evidence and decide whether the evidence supports the charges. In civil suits,

GOE 11.04.01/O*Net 28102
O*Net-Soc 23-1023.00

Judges hear the claims of the parties involved. In nonjury civil trials, these professionals make decisions regarding which party is at fault. During trials, Judges listen to the evidence that lawyers submit. They then decide whether the evidence relates to the case and whether the attorneys present the evidence in an acceptable manner. For jury cases, judicial professionals need to inform the jurors of their duties. They also explain the laws that apply to each case to the jurors.

In addition to their courtroom activities, Judges need to stay informed about changes in legislation. They spend time studying past cases that may apply to a present case. They may also perform research on legal matters relating to each case.

Judges are either elected or appointed to office, depending on the type of court. For state-level courts, most Judges are elected rather than appointed. Through this process, many states hope to make judicial officials more responsive to the needs of the general public than they may otherwise be. The length of judicial terms varies in each jurisdiction. Judges in some courts have short terms, while other professionals may serve for terms that last several years. Some Judges receive a lifetime appointment to the position.

In order to remain objective, Judges need to be free of financial, political, or social ties to the parties involved in the cases they hear. For this reason, United States federal court Judges may disqualify themselves from hearing particular cases.

Before individuals can advance to the position of a Judge, they typically need to practice law for several years. People who are interested in a judicial career may also want to read about the occupations of Lawyer (*Occupational Guidance* Vol. I, Unit 1I, No. 4), City Attorney (Vol. III, Unit 3H, No. 6), Corporate Attorney (Vol. III, Unit 2I, No. 20), Patent Attorney (Vol. III, Unit 1I, No. 12), and Public Defender (Vol. VI, Unit 3H, No. 10).

Earnings

Judges' earnings vary according to the type of judicial position they hold. The salaries of magistrates and state Judges are set locally. As a result, these professionals' incomes also vary according to their location. The median annual salary for Judges is about $94,000. Most individuals in this profession earn between $45,000 and $120,000 per year. The lowest-paid officials earn less than $24,000 a year. The highest-paid Judges earn more than $138,000 annually. State governments typically pay individuals a higher salary than local governments do.

These professionals usually receive benefits in addition to their salaries. Government agencies may provide health insurance, sick leave, paid vacation time and holidays, and retirement plans for Judges.

History of Occupation

The legal system that the United States currently uses started to develop during colonial times. The first colonists had few law enforcement officials, but they did recognize a need to maintain law and order among the people. These individuals based their government and legal systems on those of England.

Each of the colonies developed its own local laws and legal institutions. As a result, there were wide differences between the colonies' legal systems. The duties of Judges also varied between colonies. In most cases, Judges had high status positions in their communities, but their power was typically limited. People could remove the Judges from office if their rulings were unpopular with the public.

The U.S. Constitution established a federal government and the colonies became states late in the 18th century. The Constitution allowed the new states to keep much of the power they previously had as colonies. Each state developed its own system of laws and courts. They continued to include the role of Judges in their court systems

There are currently fifty-one separate systems of courts in the United States—one for each state and one for the federal government. State-level courts handle most of the judicial work in the country. Federal courts typically handle cases involving crimes committed on federal property or disputes between citizens of different states.

Working Conditions

Judges spend time in courtrooms and in a private office called a *chamber*. The facilities of the courtroom and chamber vary according to the size and financial situation of the jurisdiction. Most courtrooms and chambers are well furnished and comfortable. Judges in higher courts generally have larger chambers than those in lower courts. Some individuals in this profession work in offices or law libraries rather than in the court system.

Hours of Work

Judges often work more than fifty hours a week. They spend some time in courtrooms and the rest of their time performing other tasks, such as conducting research or consulting with the parties and attorneys involved in a case. Judges need to stay informed about laws and developments that affect their work, so they may spend time studying legal publications outside of their work hours.

Ability Required

Judges should be thoroughly knowledgeable about laws and legal developments that affect the cases they hear. They need to be able to understand complicated or detailed legal issues. These individuals should have strong analytical and listening skills. They need to be able to relate a possible solution to a problem and then determine the steps by which the solution can be accomplished. Judges should also be able to remain objective and base their judgments on facts, rather than allowing their personal prejudices or emotions to influence their decisions.

Temperament Required

Individuals in this profession should be emotionally stable and remain calm during court proceedings, regardless of hostility or resentment between opposing parties. They should stay emotionally detached from cases in order to maintain their objectivity. Judges should be patient and honest. They should also have integrity and a strong sense of ethics.

Education and Training Required

Some jurisdictions allow individuals without a law degree to have limited judicial powers. Although Judges do not necessarily need to have a law degree for some positions, they may not be able to advance in this profession without one.

For most judicial positions, candidates need to have a degree in law and be licensed to practice law. The requirements for admittance to law schools may vary depending on the school, but programs typically require applicants to have a bachelor's degree before entering the law program. Law schools may not require candidates to pursue a specific major in their undergraduate studies, however. Regardless of their major, students can benefit from taking undergraduate classes in English, speech, political science, and economics. Many people who plan to attend law school choose to major in areas such as public policy, political science, philosophy, or law.

There are several colleges and universities in the United States that offer a master's degree program in conflict-management and dispute-resolution. Individuals who pursue a *juris doctor* (JD) degree typically spend three years completing the studies necessary for this degree. Some law schools offer part-time programs for a JD degree. These programs may require four or five years of study.

Before they can practice law, graduates need to pass the bar examination of the state in which they plan to work. Prospective Judges typically need to gain several years of work experience as a lawyer before they are elected or appointed as a Judge.

Finances Required Before Earning

Students who are interested in this career should plan to pursue postsecondary education. They typically spend about four years in undergraduate school and an additional three years in law school. The cost of undergraduate tuition at public home-state universities typically ranges from $6,000 to $16,000 a year. Students from out of state may pay additional fees. At private colleges, tuition may cost from $15,000 to more than $30,000 per year. Tuition for graduate-level courses usually costs about the same as or slightly more than undergraduate tuition. Students should also budget for living expenses, which can range from $5,000 to $15,000 annually. Books and supplies may cost an additional $1,000 per year.

Financial Aid Information

For a free booklet on financial aid, one may write to or e-mail the following:

Financial Aids for Students
Finney Company
3943 Meadowbrook Road
Minneapolis, Minnesota 55426-4505
feedback@finney-hobar.com

Attractive Features

Individuals who are interested in the legal system and who enjoy resolving issues may appreciate this career. They may also appreciate the challenges and variety involved in judicial work. In addition, Judges may gain a sense of satisfaction in feeling that they are contributing to their country's justice system.

Disadvantages

Judges may find issuing judgments or determining sentences to be stressful, particularly for complicated or difficult cases. These professionals may have to handle hostility or resentment from parties involved in court proceedings. Some people in this profession dislike the amount of time they need to spend studying case histories and legal issues. Elected Judges do not have the same level of job security as appointed Judges.

Outlook for the Future

The number of employment opportunities for Judges will probably grow more slowly than the average rate of employment growth through the year 2012. Factors such as high crime rates, safety issues, and the need for the efficient administration of justice will likely contribute to the demand for Judges. Budget cuts and limited government finances will probably slow job growth, however.

Experts predict that most job openings for Judges will likely result from current Judges retiring from this profession. Many Judges are opting for early retirement. This trend should create additional job openings in this field.

Licensing, Unions, Organizations

In the United States, each state is responsible for determining its own requirements for state-level judicial candidates. Many states and precincts require Judges to have a license to practice law. Applicants for a position as a federal Judge may need to pass an examination that the U.S. Office of Personnel Management administers.

Judges typically need to become members of the state bar association. They may also choose to join professional organizations, such as the American Bar Association, the National Council of Juvenile and Family Court Judges, the American Judicature Society, and the American Judges Association.

Suggested Courses in High School

Students who are interested in this career should take college-preparatory classes in high school. Through English and speech courses, individuals can develop communication skills. In social studies classes, prospective Judges can learn about laws, law enforcement systems, and judicial systems. Many legal terms are based on the Latin language, so students who are interested in this career can benefit from taking Latin courses.

Suggested High School Activities

By participating in extracurricular activities, individuals can develop interpersonal skills and poise in their interactions with others. Prospective Judges can also gain applicable experience for this career by participating in student government activities. They can develop analytical and logical reasoning skills by joining a debate team.

Methods to Enter Work

Many law school graduates start working in a law firm or establish an independent practice. Individuals may find information about employment opportunities through their school's placement office or legal publications.

Individuals who have a few years of experience and who have developed a solid reputation may have opportunities to run for election to the position of district Judge. Candidates for such a position usually need to pay a filing fee to place their name on the ballot.

If there is a vacancy between elections, the governor of a state typically appoints someone to fill the vacancy until the next election. The judicial selection committee of the state bar association may make a recommendation. This committee bases the recommendation on suggestions that lawyers in the community have made concerning their fellow attorneys who are interested in judgeships.

Additional Information

American Judges Association
300 Newport Avenue
Williamsburg, Virginia 23185-4147
http://aja.ncsc.dni.us

Related Web Sites

American Bar Association
http://www.abanet.org
This Web site offers information about career resources, law school, public education, and related publications.

Law School Admissions Council
http://www.lsac.org
Visitors to this Web site can find information about law school forums, minority perspectives, law school rankings and resources, financial aid opportunities, and related publications and videos.

Testing Your Interests

How can you know if you are suited to this occupation? Ask yourself these questions. If you answer "yes" to most of them and the job sounds interesting, you may want to look into this vocation further as a possible career.

1. Do I enjoy working with other people?

2. Am I patient and a good listener?

3. Do I have strong analytical and decision-making skills?

4. Can I remain objective when making decisions, regardless of my personal opinions and prejudices?

Published by Finney Company, Minneapolis, Minnesota 55426-4505

Occupational Guidance

News Librarian

Description of Work

News Librarians maintain the libraries of news publications. They manage information and resources that reporters, editorial writers, and other members of the staff use when researching articles. Most news libraries contain a variety of print and electronic resources, such as access to the Internet and intranets, databases, public records, files, tapes, and microfilm.

In addition to helping staff members find and verify facts, News Librarians may provide background information that explains the relationships of news stories to previous events in the city, state, nation, and world. When unexpected events occur, including natural disasters, crimes, or sudden deaths of public officials or famous people, these librarians may supply factual and biographical material, maps, photographs, and technical data about related events and the circumstances.

Newspapers often undertake editorial campaigns on behalf of community welfare. Writers for these campaigns frequently utilize reference libraries to find statistics, data, and background material to support and substantiate their views. Reporters cannot be experts in every topic, so small papers that have one or two staff writers may especially rely on their reference library for information about various subjects. Large metropolitan daily publications may employ several librarians to manage the reference department.

News Librarians typically try to anticipate the needs of the newspaper staff and prepare for these needs in advance. If they know a significant convention or local event is going to occur, for example, they may assemble maps and photographs or write biographical sketches of the individuals involved in the event. These professionals may occasionally suggest a story that editors have overlooked. Publications often rely on library employees to notify their staff members of significant anniversaries or historical dates.

In addition to providing information for editorial writers and news reporters, librarians may supply material specifically for individual newspaper departments. For example, they may provide athletes' records and personal information for writers in the sports department. Editors of variety sections, business pages, real estate columns, Sunday departments, and other specialized sections frequently need other types of information. Libraries may also supply data from their own and other newspapers for the circulation and advertising departments.

For many large publications, the news library is centrally located in the building. Librarians may store maps, documents, and photographs in computer files. They can then transfer these files quickly to newspaper staff members. These professionals may also index current issues the newspaper has on file and archives of past editions on a computer. Through the Internet, librarians can typically access most other large daily newspapers and numerous other resources. In addition, they can use a computer to search magazines for specific information. Professionals in this field often keep journals in the library for up to one year. Many of these reference facilities maintain archived information in digital or microfiche formats to save space in the library. Using microphotography, librarians can reduce an entire page to a half-inch square of microfilm.

In response to information requests from newspaper staff members, News Librarians often compile a collection of related articles, books, and photographs or prepare a report with corresponding reference material. They may occasionally write summaries and outlines of information or explanatory notes to save the writer time. Librarians may either supervise or personally read and mark newspapers and periodicals. They may also spend time classifying, indexing, and entering information into computer files. Many individuals in this profession are responsible for maintaining records and statistics or inputting news articles into databases. They continually work to discard obsolete material as well. They should be concise and efficient in their work in order to avoid costing the newspaper money or decreasing the publication's effectiveness.

Many newspapers assign News Librarians the task of creating and maintaining an *intranet*, which is an in-house computer database of information, facts, and resources. They typically make the intranet accessible to other newspaper employees. Librarians may also share information

GOE 11.02.04/O*Net 31502A

O*Net-Soc 25-4021.00

with other organizations and access outside resources through the Internet.

In addition to their other duties, News Librarians may hire, train, and evaluate other library staff members. They often create the work schedules for employees in the reference department. These professionals are frequently responsible for selecting and purchasing reference books for the library. They may also prepare library budgets and coordinate library activities with other newspaper departments.

Individuals who are interested in this career may also want to read about related occupations, including Press Service Manager (*Occupational Guidance* Vol. VIII, Unit 1I, No. 18), Public Librarian (Vol. II, Unit 2I, No. 10), Health Sciences Librarian (Vol. II, Unit 1I, No. 20), and Library Technician (Vol. VII, Unit 2I, No. 1).

Earnings

Entry-level News Librarians who work in the library of a metropolitan daily publication usually work as a classifier or researcher. They often earn from $15,000 to $26,000 a year. Experienced librarians typically earn from $34,000 to $54,000 annually. Individuals who work as a library supervisor usually earn a salary at the high end of the pay scale. Their income may vary according to their level of experience and their employer.

In general, employees at small newspapers earn less than individuals who work for large publications. Many small newspapers maintain limited resources in their libraries. These facilities may consist of copies of previous editions and offer Internet access. They may staff part-time librarians or assign classification and research duties to other employees.

The types of benefits employees receive in addition to their salaries may vary according to the company for which they work. Most employers offer pension plans, several different kinds of insurance programs, and paid holidays and vacation time.

History of Occupation

In the early history of American newspapers, editors often kept a few reference books and a box or scrapbook of clippings available for research purposes. The *Hartford Courant*, a daily publication that began in the 1760s, accumulated books and records of official documents. The publication did not start systematically filing or indexing clippings and other material until many years later, however. The *New York Herald* and the *New York Tribune* organized some of the earliest newspaper libraries. Some newspapers did not establish libraries until the first quarter of the 20th century.

During the Spanish-American War, many newspaper editors began to recognize the need for comprehensive libraries in order to present accurate information about economic and military issues. This recognition increased when news publications reported on World War I, World War II, and the complicated patterns of postwar events.

In 1914, the *Philadelphia Public Ledger* hired Joseph Kwapil to create a news library. Kwapil had previously worked at newspapers including the *Minneapolis Tribune*, the *Chicago Tribune*, the *Philadelphia Evening Bulletin*, and the *Washington Times*. He applied information he had learned from these experiences and spent nine years establishing the library. Kwapil then started to work on developing a professional association for News Librarians.

Although many publications were unwilling to share resources at the time, with the help of five other specialists, Newspaper Librarians succeeded in organizing as an official group in 1923. Their organization became affiliated with the Special Libraries Association in 1924. The number of participants in this organization has grown steadily since that time. Present-day news libraries and reference departments often contain many different resources and technological equipment, with which News Librarians can access information from around the world.

Working Conditions

Newspaper librarians may frequently work under pressure to find information quickly so staff members can meet deadlines. Large newspapers typically provide efficient and up-to-date research equipment for these professionals to use. Individuals who work for daily publications and community newspapers usually have access to adequate storage and work space and good lighting. News Librarians may work independently on some projects and serve as a member of a team for other projects. Head librarians are typically responsible for supervising the assistants in the reference department.

Hours of Work

Most News Librarians have a standard five-day, forty-hour workweek. Many publications keep their library open every day of the week and for more than eight hours each day. Therefore, individuals who work for such publications may staff different shifts and work some weekends and in the evenings. Many newspapers divide the library staff into groups to work day or night schedules. The hours may vary from one newspaper to another. Head librarians frequently have regular daytime and weekday schedules, however. Individuals who have seniority in the department may have the first choice of work schedules.

Ability Required

News Librarians need to have a good memory. They should be thoroughly knowledgeable about library procedures. These individuals should be able to read rapidly and have excellent research skills. In order to serve as effective managers, they need to be able to organize their personal work and the work of their assistants. Librarians should also be able to train assistants in library procedures. They need to have strong interpersonal and verbal and written communication skills in order to work with reporters, editors, and their assistants. In addition, these professionals should be proficient in using computers and research software.

Temperament Required

News Librarians should be interested in current affairs. They can benefit from having a studious yet creative nature. These professionals should be detail-oriented in their work and enjoy conducting research. Librarians should also enjoy working with and helping other people. They should be conscientious in their work and willing to maintain the newspaper's standards. In addition, they should be patient, thorough, and diligent in researching different topics. These professionals need to be willing to be flexible in order to adapt to sudden changes in schedules. They need to practice discretion, especially when they work in markets that have competing newspapers.

Education and Training Required

Many news publications have started to place increasing importance on the maintenance of news libraries. In order to operate a library or reference department efficiently, News Librarians need to have technical skills and thoroughly understand the methods of this profession. Most large daily newspapers require librarians to have a minimum of a bachelor's degree, preferably in library science. Individuals who pursue a double major in journalism and library science may have an advantage over other candidates in securing a position in this field. They should also obtain a well-rounded liberal arts background. Prospective News Librarians typically take classes that focus on cataloging and classifying information, reference work and organization, administration, information science, and computer science.

Prestigious newspapers often prefer to hire candidates who have a master of library science (MLS) degree. The American Library Association currently accredits more than fifty schools that have programs in library science.

Newspaper Librarians need to have a combination of journalism and library science skills. They should stay informed about current events and developments in the technological methods of locating and retrieving information.

Finances Required Before Earning

The cost of postsecondary tuition for prospective News Librarians typically varies according to the type of school they attend. At public home-state universities, tuition may cost between $6,000 and $16,000 each year. Students from out of state may pay additional fees. At private colleges, tuition often costs from $15,000 to more than $30,000 a year. Individuals who pursue a master's degree may pay about the same as or slightly more than undergraduate students for tuition. Annual living expenses for students often range from $5,000 to $15,000. Books and supplies may cost an additional $1,000 each year.

Financial Aid Information

For a free booklet on financial aid, one may write to or e-mail the following:

Financial Aids for Students
Finney Company
3943 Meadowbrook Road
Minneapolis, Minnesota 55426-4505
feedback@finney-hobar.com

Attractive Features

Many News Librarians enjoy working in the newspaper industry. They have access to records of current and past events and can learn about various topics that affect people around the world. These professionals may have opportunities to interact with a wide range of people in their work. They frequently assist individuals who are conducting research for major news stories. Librarians also have opportunities to use their imagination and resourcefulness to trace information. They may enjoy the challenges and variety that accompany each project.

Disadvantages

Some News Librarians dislike working in the evenings and on weekends. Their work schedule may be disruptive to their family or social life. These professionals may feel frustrated or stressed when they have difficulty locating or verifying material. Reporters and other staff members who use the newspaper library typically work under heavy deadline pressure. This pressure can also affect librarians. Some individuals in this profession feel they do not receive the level of appreciation and recognition they deserve.

Outlook for the Future

As the availability of electronic information increases, Newspaper Librarians should have access to expanding resources. They will likely continue to need to have excellent information-gathering skills, especially concerning data analysis, spreadsheets, and database development. People who stay informed about developments in technological research methods and current events should have an advantage over other applicants in securing a position in this field. Job seekers may face strong competition for available jobs. News Librarians who have a master's degree may also have an advantage in the job search.

Licensing, Unions, Organizations

Some librarians become members of the Newspaper Guild or intracompany employee groups. Professionals in this field can also join the News Librarians' division of the

Special Libraries Association. This division holds meetings for News Librarians during the association's conventions. The American Library Association is another professional organization that individuals in this career field can join. This association accredits schools of library science.

Suggested Courses in High School

Prospective News Librarians should enroll in college-preparatory courses, including classes in English, mathematics, science, social studies, and a foreign language, in high school. They can benefit from taking as wide a range of subjects as possible. Through journalism and composition classes, students can develop writing skills. They can gain background knowledge for this career through history, social and political science, economics, and fine arts courses. News Librarians also need to have computer skills, so students who are interested in this career can benefit from taking computer science classes.

Suggested High School Activities

By becoming a staff member of the school newspaper, prospective News Librarian can gain applicable experience for this career. They can learn about library procedures by working in the school library after classes or during study periods. Students can increase their knowledge of various topics and develop interpersonal skills by participating in activities like student government, a debate club, a drama club, special-interest groups, and community groups. They can also gain applicable experience for this profession by visiting a public library, reviewing various reference books, and reading about a wide range of subjects.

Methods to Enter Work

Graduates of a bachelor's or master's degree program can contact their school's placement office for assistance in finding a position in this field. They can also apply directly to newspapers or other organizations that hire special librarians. Individuals may be able to learn about available positions by registering with federal, state, or private employment agencies. In addition, employers may advertise job opportunities in the classified sections of newspapers or through trade and professional publications. Some people who are interested in this career start working as front desk assistants in newspaper libraries. After they obtain training and complete the educational requirements for this career, they may have opportunities to advance to the position of News Librarian.

Additional Information

American Library Association
50 East Huron Street
Chicago, Illinois 60611
http://www.ala.org

Association for Library and Information Science Education
PO Box 4219
Oak Ridge, Tennessee 37830
http://www.alise.org

Newspaper Guild
501 Third Street NW, Suite 250
Washington, DC 20001
http://www.newsguild.org

Special Libraries Association
331 South Patrick Street
Alexandria, Virginia 22314-3501
http://www.sla.org

Related Web Sites

NewsliBlog
http://newslib.blogspot.com
Viewers of this Web site can find archives, professional development information, occupational news, and links to News Librarian blogs about related information.

Special Libraries Association News Division
http://www.ibiblio.org/slanews
This membership-based Web site is associated with the Special Libraries Association. Nonmember viewers can access articles, related resources and links, and career profiles at this Web site.

Testing Your Interests

How can you know if you are suited to this occupation? Ask yourself these questions. If you answer "yes" to most of them and the job sounds interesting, you may want to look into this vocation further as a possible career.

1. Am I thorough, accurate, and detail-oriented in my work?

2. Am I interested in current affairs and various news topics?

3. Do I enjoy working with and helping other people?

4. Do I enjoy finding and researching specific information?

5. Can I read rapidly and understand the significance of and connection between information resources?

Published by Finney Company, Minneapolis, Minnesota 55426-4505
© Finney Company 2005

Occupational Guidance

Piano Technician

Description of Work

Piano Technicians, also called piano tuner-technicians, tune, repair, and adjust pianos to keep the instruments in good condition. They may work on a range of pianos, from instruments that need to be slightly adjusted to pianos that require a great deal of repair work. These professionals may work on pianos for organizations such as major symphony orchestras, churches, and schools or for individuals who play the instrument for their own entertainment. Technicians may also recondition or rebuild pianos.

Tuning a piano is an exacting process. Technicians can tune pianos in the same way other stringed instruments are tuned. They tighten or loosen the instrument's strings to produce a flat or sharp pitch. These professionals need to manipulate a tuning lever when they adjust the piano's strings. They typically use the lever with all eighty-eight keys on the instrument, working from octave to octave. Each key has from one to three strings. If a string is out of tune, it produces a small pulsation, or beat. Technicians tune each string separately in order to achieve the correct pitch.

Some Piano Technicians use a tuning fork to set the pitch of the first string, while other individuals in this profession choose to tune each string by ear. Technicians can also use an electronic tuner. This device indicates the musical position of a particular string as it relates to the standard of the electronic tuner. Technicians cannot typically achieve an exact or perfect pitch, however. They may instead tune some pianos to the player's preference. For example, a concert pianist may prefer a piano to be tuned so that the highest notes are slightly sharp.

Technicians start by tuning one note, usually Middle C or the A below it in the middle octave. They strike the key to assess its tone. These professionals then tighten or loosen the tuning pins until the string produces a clear tone and achieves the correct pitch. After the first note, individuals tune all the notes relative to one another in the *temperament octave,* which extends from the F below Middle C to the F above Middle C. They then tune the remaining strings up and down the piano. Technicians use the notes in the temperament octave as the standard for the other strings.

When individuals tune a piano by ear, they do not listen to the note musically or try to determine whether the strings sound sharp or flat. Instead, they play two strings at the same time and listen for interference beats, which occur when any two close musical tones are slightly out of tune. They may need to repeat this procedure for each string at least twice and possibly more times in order to accurately tune the piano.

When Piano Technicians work on an instrument that is tuned regularly, they may only need to raise or lower the pitch of the piano slightly, depending on whether the pitch is flat or sharp overall. For pianos that have not been tuned for a long period of time, these professionals typically need to raise the pitch. Pianos that have not been tuned for several years may be flat by as much as half a step. Individuals may need to tune such a piano up to three times in order to achieve the correct pitch. If strings break during the process or tuning pins become loose, these professionals need to replace or repair the strings or pins.

Depending on the technician's preferences and technical abilities as well as the needs of the local market, an individual in this profession may also perform other types of piano maintenance jobs. For example, a technician may splice or replace broken strings, test and adjust a piano's pedal action, fix misaligned hammers or other action parts, regulate the action, or make any other repairs an instrument needs. Some professionals in this field own and operate a piano rebuilding shop. People who own pianos can take their instrument to this shop for major repair work. When technicians perform rebuilding work, they may restring the piano, replace pin blocks, replace hammers and other action parts, replace wooden bridges, fix cracked soundboards, realign or replace action components, and recover keyboards. They may also refinish an instrument. Some technicians specialize in restoring player pianos or antique pianos. Professionals in this field may also offer assessment services. They base the assessment of a piano's value on the instrument's age, condition, quality, and brand.

Individuals who are interested in this career may also want to read about related occupations, including Piano

GOE 05.05.12/O*Net 85921A
O*Net-Soc 49-9063.01

Stringer (*Occupational Guidance* Vol. V, Unit 5H, No. 18), Electronic Keyboard Technician (Vol. VI, Unit 5H, No. 12), and Stringed Instrument Repairer (Vol. II, Unit 5H, No. 11).

Earnings

Piano Technicians' earnings frequently vary according to their level of experience. These individuals' workload may fluctuate seasonally. The average income for full-time employees of piano tuning companies may range from about $23,000 to $45,000 a year. Most Piano Technicians are self-employed, however. These individuals often charge between $80 and $120 for a tuning. They may earn from $35,000 to more than $50,000 a year if they work full-time.

Full-time employees of piano tuning companies may receive benefits in addition to their salaries. Companies often provide health insurance, sick leave, and paid holidays and vacation time. Self-employed technicians typically need to provide for their own benefits out of their earnings.

History of Occupation

The dulcimer was the forerunner of the piano. This instrument was popular in the 14th century. Individuals played this small, rectangular-shaped stringed instrument with two mallets. They held one mallet in each hand.

In the 15th century, people started playing the clavichord. This instrument, named for *clavis*, meaning *key*, and *chord*, meaning *string*, was the first true keyboard instrument. The clavichord was basically a dulcimer with a keyboard. People could not produce a loud tone with the clavichord, so they limited its use to home entertainment and small chamber concerts.

In the 16th century, the harpsichord was introduced. The harpsichord is more closely related to the psaltery than to the modern piano. The psaltery was a stringed instrument that people played by plucking the strings with their fingers. Players also plucked the strings of the harpsichord, but this instrument involved keyboard action as well. The harpsichord could produce a louder tone than the clavichord, but it was unable to produce subtle gradations of sound.

The development of the *pianoforte*, or piano, solved this problem. In 1709, Italian harpsichord maker, Bartolommeo Cristofori, replaced the jacks of the harpsichord with hammers, which controlled the loudness and softness of the instrument. He named his invention *gravecembalo col piano e forte*, which was eventually shortened to the word *piano*. The piano was an improvement over the clavichord in that players could sustain notes as long as they wanted. They could also play both loud and soft tones on the piano.

In the late 18th century, the piano became the accepted keyboard instrument. The piano was mechanically complex, so individuals could not tune their pianos as easily as clavichord and harpsichord players could tune their instruments. To meet the demand for piano tuning services, some people started working as professional Piano Technicians. The need

for tuning services continues. Present-day technicians may adjust a piano, make repairs, and rebuild or restore a piano in addition to tuning the instrument.

Working Conditions

Piano Technicians work in a variety of indoor settings. They visit people's homes and other facilities, including dance halls, concert halls, schools, or churches, to tune pianos. Some piano owners leave technicians alone to perform the tuning work. In other homes or facilities, professionals in this field may interact with adults, children, or pets while they tune or repair a piano. Some technicians work exclusively in shops or factories, but most individuals in this profession travel from one location to another to tune pianos. The specific environment in which they work varies from location to location. Some work environments may be cluttered or dusty.

Hours of Work

Piano Technicians perform most of their work during regular business hours, from about 9:00 a.m. to 5:00 p.m., Monday through Friday. These individuals typically have some flexibility in their schedule, especially if they are self-employed. To meet the needs of customers, they may occasionally work in the evenings or on weekends. They may also work into the evening to complete a project. If they encounter broken strings or other complications when tuning a piano, these professionals customarily continue working until they repair the strings or fix the other problems. People who work part-time as piano tuners may frequently tune and repair pianos in the evenings. In general, technicians are especially busy during the fall and winter months when people start to focus on indoor activities like piano playing.

Ability Required

Piano Technicians need to have good hearing and an excellent sense of vibration and pitch. They should have good manual dexterity and hand-eye coordination. Although pianos are large, they are also delicate. Technicians need to move their hands carefully and efficiently when they tune strings and when they mute the strings they are not tuning.

Professionals in this field should be able to concentrate for extended periods of time and consistently perform high quality work. They can benefit from having an aptitude for mechanics and mathematics. They should also have good organizational and communication skills. Self-employed technicians can benefit from having business skills.

Temperament Required

Piano Technicians are typically self-sufficient and enjoy practical, manual work. They should be patient when tuning or repairing a piano. These individuals may need to spend a great deal of time adjusting strings to achieve the correct tone. They should also be patient when they interact with customers.

Technicians often rely on referrals to increase their business. Therefore, they should present a friendly, courteous, and helpful demeanor when they talk with customers. They should be self-confident and enthusiastic about their work.

Education and Training Required

People usually spend from five months to two years training for this career. During this training period, they often obtain a combination of classroom instruction and practical experience in the areas of piano tuning and repair.

In the United States, a few career and technical schools and community colleges offer programs in piano technology. Private schools that have musical instrument repair programs may also teach students how to tune pianos and other instruments. In the classroom, students typically learn about basic tuning techniques and receive detailed instruction about small repair procedures. In some classes, students may learn how to rebuild an entire piano, which involves installing new strings, new hammers, new keys, and recovered keys. Participants of these programs also have opportunities to obtain practical experience working on pianos in need of tuning. Once they graduate from such programs, individuals usually work as assistants to experienced technicians for some time before they advance to the position of Piano Technician.

Some Piano Technicians obtain training for this career through correspondence courses, seminars, conventions, and independent study. Other technicians train for this profession by working for several years as an apprentice or assistant to an experienced technician.

Finances Required Before Earning

Individuals who train for this career by working as an assistant to an experienced technician need to have enough money to pay for their living expenses until they receive their first paycheck. In contrast, some people prepare for this career through independent study and correspondence courses. Such courses may cost $1,000 or more.

Other prospective technicians choose to attend a career and technical school or community college. At public institutions, tuition usually costs between $2,000 and $7,000 a year. Private career and technical schools may charge from $4,000 to $15,000 annually for tuition. Students should also budget for living expenses, which frequently range from $5,000 to $15,000 a year. Books and supplies may cost about $1,000 each year.

People who want to become self-employed need to purchase the necessary tools and equipment. They may spend several hundreds of dollars on the basic tools for this career. Computerized tuners, office equipment, and cellular phones may cost several thousands of dollars. Individuals who want to open a repair shop may need to invest tens of thousands of dollars for the shop facility and other equipment.

Financial Aid Information

For a free booklet on financial aid, one may write to or e-mail the following:

Financial Aids for Students
Finney Company
3943 Meadowbrook Road
Minneapolis, Minnesota 55426-4505
feedback@finney-hobar.com

Attractive Features

Many Piano Technicians appreciate the opportunities that accompany this career to meet a wide variety of people. Individuals in this profession may feel a sense of satisfaction and accomplishment when they complete a project and please a customer. Technicians typically perform a variety of tasks in a range of locations throughout their workday. Self-employed professionals can set their own schedule and pace of work.

Disadvantages

Some technicians dislike having to move from one location to another to perform their work. Individuals in this profession may need to travel in bad weather conditions at times. Some people dislike having to continuously interact with strangers. They may feel frustrated if children or adults distract or interrupt them when they are tuning a piano.

Outlook for the Future

This occupation is relatively small compared to many other professions. Sales of new pianos have decreased in recent years. This factor may slow job growth for Piano Technicians. People will likely continue to use older pianos, including antique pianos and player pianos, however. As a result, the demand for technicians to tune, repair, and rebuild the instruments will also likely continue. Candidates for a position in this field will likely find some job openings as current technicians transfer to other occupations or retire from the workforce. Self-employed professionals who tune and repair instruments for individuals, schools, churches, and other facilities will likely find the strongest market in this field.

Licensing, Unions, Organizations

Piano Technicians do not typically join unions. Many of these individuals choose to become members of professional organizations, however. For example, they may join the Piano Technicians Guild, which provides educational opportunities for its members through conventions, seminars, and local chapter meetings. The guild also offers a certification program. Individuals who pass a series of examinations on a broad range of topics, including tuning, repair, action regulation, and piano structure, can earn the title of Registered Piano Technician. In addition to professional organizations, many technicians choose to become members of community associations.

Suggested Courses in High School

Prospective Piano Technicians can benefit from taking music classes in high school. Through classes in mathematics and physics, these individuals may learn about the basic theories involved in tuning a piano. They can develop manual dexterity and other skills for this career by taking courses in industrial technology, particularly woodworking classes. Individuals who plan to be self-employed can benefit from enrolling in business and computer classes. Through courses in public speaking, students can develop communication skills.

Suggested High School Activities

Students who are interested in this career may want to participate in music-related activities, such as the school marching or concert band, an orchestra, or a choir. They may also benefit from taking private piano lessons. Through a part-time job in a retail establishment, prospective technicians can develop their customer service skills. Students can learn about this profession by observing Piano Technicians at work.

Methods to Enter Work

Self-employed technicians with limited experience may have difficulty securing jobs, because many people want experienced Piano Technicians to work on their instruments. Individuals may be able to gain experience in this field by working as an apprentice at a music store or with an established technician. Students at a career and technical school or community college can often find information about technicians in their area through their school's placement office. Trade journals or professional organizations may also provide information about established Piano Technicians. Some piano factories and colleges hire technicians, but these facilities typically prefer to employ experienced individuals. Once they are established in this field, self-employed technicians often advertise their services in newspapers or trade journals.

Additional Information

Piano Technicians Guild
4444 Forest Avenue
Kansas City, Missouri 66106
http://www.ptg.org

Related Web Sites

History of the Piano Forte
http://www.uk-piano.org/history/history.html
Viewers of this Web site can learn about the history of the piano and piano tuning, including the instrument's evolution, the different types and brands of pianos, and composers of piano music. They can also access links to related Web sites and information about book resources.

Pianoland.com
http://www.pianoland.com
This resource allows viewers to sign up for a free newsletter that features information about pianos and related products. The Web site also allows individuals to access a learning center and a resource page with piano-care tips.

Robert G. Kelly: Piano Tuning & Repair
http://www.pianotuner.com
This Web site provides information about piano care and service, piano evaluation, proper ways to move a piano, and related facts and information.

Testing Your Interests

How can you know if you are suited to this occupation? Ask yourself these questions. If you answer "yes" to most of them and the job sounds interesting, you may want to look into this vocation further as a possible career.

1. Do I enjoy music, especially piano music?
2. Do I have good hearing and an excellent sense of pitch?
3. Do I have an aptitude for mechanical work?
4. Am I patient and careful in my work?
5. Am I willing to travel to different locations to perform my work?
6. Am I comfortable interacting with strangers on a daily basis?

Published by Finney Company, Minneapolis, Minnesota 55426-4505
© Finney Company 2005

Occupational Guidance

Tile Setter

Description of Work

Many residential and commercial buildings have tiled floors and walls. Building owners may choose to install tile because the material withstands hard wear and requires less care and attention than many other surfaces. Water does not harm tiled surfaces. As a result, people often use this material in areas such as patios, tunnels, lobbies, bathrooms, and kitchens that may frequently be exposed to water.

Tile Setters are professional tile installers. Many individuals in this field work for masonry, stonework, floor work, and carpentry contractors. Other individuals are self-employed. In the initial steps of a project, Tile Setters typically select which materials to use and determine the amount they need of each material for a particular job. They may work with various types of tile, including ceramic, porcelain, slate, granite, limestone, glass, or marble.

At the beginning of a project, Tile Setters estimate the number of tiles they need to cover the surface. They measure the wall or floor. With these measurements, they can calculate the estimate according to the size of tile the customer wants. Tile Setters may order additional tiles to match patterns, make designs, and fix cracked or chipped areas. They also consider the requirements of preparing the floor or wall assembly so the area is suitable for tile installation. Setters who work for a contractor or retail tile merchant typically obtain materials directly from their employing company. They may need to place a special order if a customer wants a color or pattern that the company does not keep in stock.

Setters typically draw a level line along the top edge of the space they are going to tile. From this line, they can determine a true perpendicular line. Tile Setters use these guides to mark the approximate center of the area they are going to cover. They usually work out from this center in order to make sure the rows of tiles are straight and level. They reserve cut tiles for spaces at the ends of the surface.

When professionals install ceramic tile on a wall, they may use the *mud-set method*. With this method, they first hang wire lath or mesh on the wall to serve as a base. They nail the lath or mesh securely in place so it can hold the weight of the mortar and tiles. Tile Setters then mix the cement plaster, or *mud*. They spread, or *float*, an even coat of the mud on the lath using a trowel and other hand tools. They need to smooth and scratch the plaster carefully so the tiles fit flatly on the surface.

In most installations, however, setters install *backerboards*. They adhere the tile to the backerboards, rather than to a combination of lath or mesh and mud. Backerboards can be made of various materials, including cement, fiber cement, fiber-reinforced cement, and glass-coated gypsum boards.

For certain types of wall surfaces that are particularly suitable for tile, setters may not install lath, mesh, or backerboards. Instead, they use a *thin set* or *mastic* adhering material. They clean the wall thoroughly to remove any grease, dirt, or other substances that could prevent the material from setting properly. If there is any wallpaper on the surface, setters need to remove this paper; otherwise, the weight of the tile could eventually pull the paper from the wall and weaken the adhesive holding the tiles.

On floors or flat surfaces, setters can spread the mastic or thin set adhesive to the prepared surface. They cover a small portion of the surface at a time with the flat side of a trowel. They then comb the adhesive with the notched edge of the trowel. The ridges they create by combing the adhesive help eliminate air bubbles and make a good gripping surface for the tiles.

After they have applied the mud, backerboard, mastic, or thin set material, setters work row by row to press each tile carefully into place. They use special tools to trim tiles to fit around pipes, fixtures, doorframes, or other openings. If the tile has a design or pattern, they need to pay close attention to these details. For many projects, these professionals install a different color of tile for the border. They typically use edge tiles along exposed edges. Setters need to wipe off any excess mortar or mastic before the material hardens. When they have finished a surface, they clean it with a damp cloth to remove any particles of adhesive or any streaks or dust.

GOE 05.05.01/O*Net 87308
O*Net-Soc 47-2044.00

After setting all the tiles, individuals in this profession finish the surfaces by grouting the joints between the tiles. They use a rubber grout float to rub grout, which is a thick finishing paste, between the tiles. Setters then remove any excess material with a damp cloth or sponge. The grout helps smooth the joints and also prevents moisture from seeping behind the tiles and loosening them.

When they set plastic tiles on walls, Tile Setters use similar methods as they use for other types of tiling projects. Plastic is lightweight, so it does not need a lath base, however. Setters can apply mastic and tiles directly to prepared surfaces. They set each tile into place and press firmly on the four corners to secure it.

Individuals who specialize in installing resilient floor coverings perform many of the same steps as other professionals do when they set tile. For resilient floor coverings, setters often need to first remove the old flooring. They use machinery that has been developed specifically for this purpose. These professionals need to make the floor as level as possible. Therefore, they may nail down any loose boards or clean the existing surface so it can serve as a base. They may also install plywood on top of the original floor to provide a level work surface. For some projects, setters glue lining felt onto the plywood or subflooring. They then use a roller to press out any air bubbles and make the felt lie flat.

These professionals work from the center of the floor in much the same way as they would if they were installing tiles. They usually mark perpendicular lines on the floor. After spreading the adhesive on the surface, they position the edge of the flooring sheet along the perpendicular line. Setters then smooth the material to fit the surface. They need to take careful measurements and make adjustments for patterns. These individuals can then fit another section of sheeting snugly against the first. When they have finished the entire floor, they use a heavy roller to flatten the flooring and make sure each inch of the material is secure. These professionals may then install cove or baseboard molding to seal the joints between the floor and walls.

People who are interested in this career may also want to read about other construction-related occupations, including Floor Covering Installer (*Occupational Guidance* Vol. I, Unit 5H, No. 17), Bricklayer (Vol. VIII, Unit 1I, No. 2), and Cement Mason and Terrazzo Worker (Vol. VII, Unit 3H, No. 13).

Earnings

Unions that represent Tile Setters often set wages for their members. In most cases, nonunion employees earn about the same as union members. They may receive different benefits depending on their union status, however. In general, entry-level Tile Setters earn from about $27,000 to $33,000 a year. Experienced professionals in this field may earn from $40,000 to more than $50,000 annually. Individuals in apprenticeship programs initially receive about half the wages of entry-level Tile Setters.

Most employers provide some benefits to full-time Tile Setters in addition to their wages. Unions typically negotiate benefits for their members. Employers often provide health insurance; paid sick leave, vacation time, and holidays; and a retirement plan. Nonunion employees may receive similar benefits as union members. Self-employed Tile Setters need to arrange and pay for their own benefits.

History of Occupation

The word *ceramic* is derived from the Greek word *keramos*, which refers to a vessel made of baked clay or pottery. Researchers have determined the age of one piece of found ceramic pottery to be at least 10,000 years old. This item is still in good condition. People throughout the world, including native North and South Americans, have practiced ceramic crafts for centuries.

People eventually started to use ceramic tiles when they built homes and other structures. The Persians made highly decorative wall tiles as early as the 12th century.

Many houses in southern Europe were paved with red brick tiles. Manufacturers baked the tiles until they were hard. They sometimes glazed the tiles as well. Europeans started to use enameled tiles in the 15th and 16th centuries for paving the interiors of certain rooms, such as chapels or great rooms.

The production of tiles and related products is one of the oldest industries in the world. Technology did not significantly impact this industry until the 20th century, however. After World War II, people started to use other types of materials instead of tiles to build and finish their homes. The costs of producing tiles started to increase. As a result, many tile manufacturers started to invest in research activity to improve the efficiency and cost-effectiveness of their production processes.

Many people use decorative tiles for the walls and floors of their homes or other structures. They can purchase tiles in various colors, styles, and shapes. Manufacturers may use many different types of materials to produce tiles. Tile Setters specialize in hand setting and installing these tiles in people's homes, businesses, and other facilities.

Working Conditions

Tile Setters may work on projects ranging from new construction to remodeling jobs in both commercial and residential projects. These individuals install tiles on walls and floors in kitchens, bathrooms, vestibules, and family rooms. They may also install tile in facilities such as power plants, creameries, and swimming pools. These professionals' work sites are often dusty. Many construction sites are not heated or air-conditioned.

Hours of Work

Setters who work for contractors usually have regular forty-hour, five-day workweeks. They often start work at about 8:00 a.m. and end their workday at about 4:30 p.m.

These professionals typically have morning, lunch, and afternoon breaks. During peak business times, employers may ask Tile Setters to work overtime in order to finish jobs. These employees usually receive one-and-one-half times their regular wage for overtime hours. During times of economic downturns, individuals in this profession may be subject to layoffs.

Ability Required

Tile Setters need to have good manual dexterity and be skilled in working with their hands. They should be able to effectively use various types of tools. These professionals should have good vision in order to cut and fit each tile neatly. They need to be able to judge distances accurately and determine whether a surface is level. Tile Setters should be physically able to lift, bend, stoop, and kneel throughout the course of their workday.

Temperament Required

Tile Setters should be methodical, patient, and accurate in their work. They should enjoy working with their hands. This job may become somewhat tedious and repetitive at times; professionals in this field need to continue to prioritize quality work despite the repetitiveness of some tasks. Tile Setters often work closely with other people. They should interact well with others and be team-oriented. These individuals often work without direct supervision, so they need to be dependable, self-motivated, and responsible in order to finish their work on time.

Education and Training Required

Prospective Tile Setters may train for this career through a three-year apprenticeship program. Such programs typically combine on-the-job training with classroom studies. Apprentices may learn about blueprint reading, mathematics, materials, tools, and laying techniques during their training.

Candidates for an apprenticeship program may face a high level of competition. Therefore, many people who want to enter this career start working as finishers, or assistants, with experienced Tile Setters. Entry-level finishers are often responsible for tasks such as stocking materials and performing grout and finishing work. After they obtain experience over a period of months or years, they may learn to mix and apply cement and mastic. They can then progress to tasks such as cutting and installing tile. Most employers prefer to hire candidates for a position as a finisher who have a minimum of a high school diploma or the equivalent and who have taken basic mathematics and industrial technology courses.

Finances Required Before Earning

Employers typically pay apprentices and finishers while they obtain training. Individuals who enter this profession need to have enough money to pay for their living expenses until they receive their first paycheck. They also need

to purchase durable work clothes and comfortable shoes. Employers usually provide the necessary hand tools and equipment. People who start their own business need to pay for equipment and startup expenses, which could cost several thousand dollars.

Attractive Features

People who enjoy working with their hands may appreciate this occupation. Individuals who plan to enter this profession do not need to pay for postsecondary education; instead, they earn money while they obtain training. Many Tile Setters gain a sense of satisfaction when they complete a tiling project. They may appreciate the opportunities to complete a variety of projects and work in different locations. Experienced individuals may have opportunities to start their own business.

Disadvantages

Tile Setters may be subject to layoffs or decreased work hours during economic downturns. Individuals who want to train for this career through an apprenticeship may face a great deal of competition for entrance into such programs. This work can be physically strenuous; Tile Setters typically kneel while they perform many tasks. Some people find this work monotonous or repetitive at times.

Outlook for the Future

As growth in the number of residential, commercial, and other construction projects such as hospitals and schools continues to increase, there should be a continued demand for experienced Tile Setters. This occupation typically has a low turnover rate, however, which could negatively affect the number of available positions in the field. People may choose to use prefabricated wall and flooring products, such as fiberglass enclosures and plastic-based sheeting, for some construction projects. This factor may also slow the growth of the employment market for Tile Setters. Experienced individuals will likely continue to have an advantage over other candidates in securing a position in this field.

Licensing, Unions, Organizations

Some profesionals in this field join unions. The United Brotherhood of Carpenters and Joiners of America and the International Union of Bricklayers and Allied Craftworkers are two organizations that represent Tile Setters. Individuals in this career field can also choose to join professional organizations, including the Ceramic Tile Institute of America and the National Tile Contractors Association. There are no licensing requirements for Tile Setters.

Suggested Courses in High School

Individuals who plan to pursue a career as a Tile Setter should take industrial technology and basic mathematics courses in high school. They can particularly benefit from classes in drafting, blueprinting, and carpentry. Through art courses, students may be able to develop a good sense of color and design. Through physical education classes, prospective Tile Setters may be able to develop good coordination and build physical strength.

Suggested High School Activities

Tile Setters need to have physical stamina. Students can build stamina by participating in team and individual athletic activities. They may be able to improve their manual dexterity by completing craft projects and joining hobby clubs. Some tile contractors hire high school students to work part-time or during the summer as assistants to Tile Setters. Individuals who obtain such positions can gain applicable experience for this career.

Methods to Enter Work

Candidates for a position in this field can contact tile contractors directly to learn about employment opportunities. Some contractors keep a list of people who are interested in a position as an apprentice or finisher. These employers may then call the people on the list when openings occur. The state employment agency or apprenticeship office may also be able to provide information about opportunities in this field.

Additional Information

International Union of Bricklayers and Allied Craftworkers
International Masonry Institute
Apprenticeship and Training
1776 Eye Street NW
Washington, DC 20006
http://www.bacweb.org

United Brotherhood of Carpenters and Joiners of America
101 Constitution Avenue NW
Washington, DC 20001
http://www.carpenters.org

Related Web Sites

FloorsTransformed: Ceramic Tile Projects & Resources
http://floorstransformed.com
Viewers of this Web site can find tutorials for common tile projects, information about tools and hardware, a forum, and related resources.

The Tile Doctor
http://www.thetiledoctor.com
The Ceramic Tile Institute sponsors this Web site. Viewers can find directions for self-installation of tiles, maintenance and cleaning tips, industry and product information, a glossary, and a tile calculator.

Testing Your Interests

How can you know if you are suited to this occupation? Ask yourself these questions. If you answer "yes" to most of them and the job sounds interesting, you may want to look into this vocation further as a possible career.

1. Do I enjoy performing manual tasks?

2. Can I perform quality work despite the repetitiveness of the tasks involved in a project?

3. Do I have an aptitude for measuring distances and using tools?

4. Do I have a good sense of color, design, and space?

5. Can I be accurate and careful in my work?

Published by Finney Company, Minneapolis, Minnesota 55426-4505

Occupational Guidance

Investment Analyst

Description of Work

Investment Analysts help corporations and communities finance their expansion and growth. They assist in underwriting the sale of new issues of securities for specific amounts of money. In the underwriting process, these professionals assess, manage, and arrange sales of stocks and bonds to investors to raise the funds their clients need to complete a project. The purchasers of bonds receive repayment with interest, while the purchasers of company stocks receive payment from dividends and own shares in the company. Investment Analysts can work for a variety of employers, including insurance companies, security firms, banks, and organizations that handle mutual-pension plan investment funds.

When analysts arrange large-scale financing, they typically complete the process in several steps. They may start by analyzing the investment projects and objectives. These professionals then evaluate short-term debt securities. They usually analyze various financial reports before they recommend investment opportunities.

In an example of the financing process, the officers of a corporation may decide they need additional money for expansion, for new product development, for research, or for another reason. To secure this money, they may decide on a new stock issue. The officers then contact an Investment Analyst, who meets with the company treasurer and other financial officers. They discuss the kind and amount of stock to issue, the reason for the additional capital outlay, and other details of the transaction.

The analyst needs to determine whether the proposed expansion or improvement is sensible and logical. This professional assesses whether the project is a good risk, because the analyst does not want to promote the sale of stock in a company that is likely to lose money in the future. The specialist analyzes the company's financial statements, commodity prices, sales, costs, expenses, and tax rates. This individual also determines the organization's current value and projects its future earnings. The analyst needs to decide whether the market conditions are favorable for the sale of the type and amount of stock the company plans to

issue. In order to make such a judgment, this professional studies the industry and its products, evaluates the company's competition, and assesses current trends in business practices. The Investment Analyst may consult with several experts, including engineers, lawyers, market analysts, and consumer researchers, before reaching a conclusion. These planning, analysis, counseling, and investigative processes may take many months.

Once the investment bank agrees to the arrangements to sell the securities, the company is granted the funds to proceed with the proposed improvement or expansion. The Investment Analyst may assist with the sale of the stock by helping the investment bank find investors who are willing to buy large amounts of the stock. Banks are often especially interested in selling stock to institutional investors, such as insurance companies or mutual funds. In addition to being convenient and profitable, the purchase of large sales of stock by well-known and respected institutional investors often encourages private investors to buy the stock, which can increase the stock's value.

Investment Analysts also help arrange for the sale of bonds for cities, townships, or school districts. For example, a community may need money for road or highway construction, new schools, recreational facilities, or other improvements. If taxpayers approve the expenditures, the community may obtain the funds by a bond issue. An Investment Analyst investigates the financial stability of the community and the marketability of the bonds. If the professional deems the project a good risk, this individual underwrites the issue. Investors throughout the United States or in foreign countries may purchase these types of bonds.

Large utility companies, such as power, water, and gas suppliers, frequently rely on the services of Investment Analysts. These organizations usually have large and expensive facilities. Expansion or improvement projects for the facilities often cost many millions of dollars. Financial organizations may bid for opportunities to handle the securities of utility companies. When they place bids, they need to be thoroughly experienced and knowledgeable about the market. If an analyst places a bid that is too low, the individual might lose money, rather than make a profit. In contrast,

GOE 11.06.03/O*Net 25315

O*Net-Soc 13-2051.00

if the professional places a bid that is too high, the utility company may choose to use the services of another analyst who offers a lower bid.

In addition, Investment Analysts may regularly arrange for the sale and purchase of securities for some large investors. These professionals may work to maintain a favorable combination of different types of stocks and bonds to achieve the greatest financial return and safety for the investors. Analysts who assume this role may work as the manager or consultant for the investment portfolio of a large trust fund; a mutual fund, which is an investment fund that allows small investors to buy stock and own a variety of securities; or an insurance company. These individuals may also be involved in constructing portfolios for individuals, endowments, and nonprofit organizations.

Individuals who are interested in this career may also want to read about related occupations, including Bank Trust Officer (*Occupational Guidance* Vol. VI, Unit 4H, No. 7), Financial Planner (Vol. III, Unit 3H, No. 1), Securities Sales Agent (Vol. III, Unit 5H, No. 20), and Correspondent Bank Officer (Vol. I, Unit 5H, No. 4).

Earnings

Most people enter a career in the banking industry as a trainee. The earnings for trainees typically vary according to their level of education and experience and the size and location of the financial institution for which they work. In large companies that have assets of more than one billion dollars, trainees with a bachelor's degree often earn between $36,000 and $41,000 a year. Individuals who have a master's degree may earn a starting salary ranging from $41,000 to $51,000 annually. Experienced analysts who work for large institutions frequently earn from $57,000 to more than $90,000 a year. In addition, increasing numbers of analysts are working as independent consultants. These individuals may earn more than $120,000 each year.

Most employers in this field provide benefits to full-time analysts, in addition to their earnings. These professionals may receive paid vacation time, insurance plans, and retirement benefits.

History of Occupation

The financial lending industry in the United States grew slowly after the American Revolution. Government agencies, new banks, and railroad companies primarily used lending services to make internal improvements. Stephen Girard and David Parish were two of the earliest American financial backers. They bought $16 million in bonds from the government to help finance the Revolutionary War. In the 1830s, the United States Bank of Pennsylvania became one of the first incorporated commercial banks to enter the investment business. One of the major functions of the early investment banks was to finance railroads.

An economic depression in the 1830s caused business to slow down in the United States. People began to recognize a need to reform the securities industry. During this period, organizations obtained some investment funding from lotteries. They also relied on professional auctioneers to handle sales of securities and bonds. Before the Civil War, however, agents of foreign banking houses handled most investments.

The demand for capital that resulted from the Civil War increased the roles of American investment institutions. The industry at this time was relatively small, but it had also become sophisticated and specialized.

Between 1890 and World War I, the railroads lost their dominant position in the investment banking industry. Instead, industrial organizations, utility companies, and foreign governments became the major recipients of investment funding. In the first decade of the 20th century, President Theodore Roosevelt's administration investigated trusts and securities. The investigation resulted in new state laws and regulations regarding investments. Despite the regulations, the investment industry continued to grow and speculate into the 1920s. In 1929, the stock market crashed. Many banks closed as a result. In the 1930s, the government conducted the Gray Pecora investigation in an effort to improve the irregularities of the investment industry. This investigation resulted in the creation of the Securities Act of 1933, the establishment of the Securities and Exchange Commission, and the development of many new regulations for the investment industry.

In the period from 1932 until World War II, the investment industry underwent many readjustments. Growth in utility companies, particularly organizations that provided natural gas, telephone service, and electric power, helped increase investment activities throughout most of the century. By the 1990s, new technology and the growth of many Internet companies created a period of unprecedented stock market gains. The market was saturated with speculative, high-risk "junk" bonds, however. This saturation and the resulting deflation of the market led to another readjustment of the financial industry.

Many present-day companies and organizations rely on investment banks and Investment Analysts to obtain the funding they need for expansion and improvement projects. Analysts help assess the risk of such projects and promote positive financial growth for both companies and investors.

Working Conditions

Investment Analysts usually have a comfortable and well-equipped office. They may frequently travel to different locations within their community or the country to analyze projects. These professionals often interact with officers of corporations and community leaders.

Hours of Work

Although most banks and other financial institutions operate during regular business hours, Investment Analysts may work much more than forty hours a week. These individuals may complete paperwork, review or create reports, or attend meetings in the evenings and on weekends. They often work sixty hours or more each week.

Ability Required

Individuals in this profession need to have strong analytical and decision-making skills. They should have an aptitude for working with mathematical and financial concepts. Analysts also need to have excellent sales and communication skills. They should be able to persuade others to make investments or adopt new plans. In addition, analysts should have good judgment in recognizing market situations and projecting future trends. They should have strong technical skills and be able to use spreadsheet and statistical software.

Temperament Required

Analysts should be self-confident and be comfortable making decisions. These professionals should enjoy working with others. They need to handle pressure well and remain calm during stressful situations. Investment Analysts often have irregular schedules; they should adapt well to changes and different environments. These individuals need to remain objective in analyzing projects. They should be willing to take risks but be cautious, thorough, and detail-oriented in evaluating the risks. In addition, professionals in this field should be honest and have high ethical standards and integrity.

Education and Training Required

Many brokerage houses require applicants for a position in this field to have a graduate-level degree. Most individuals enter this career with a master in business administration (MBA) degree. Other employers may consider candidates who have a bachelor's degree, at least five years of business or finance-related experience, and some level of advanced training in investment analysis.

Prospective Investment Analysts often major in finance, economics, business administration, statistics, or accounting during their undergraduate studies. Individuals who are interested in this career can also benefit from obtaining an educational background in law and experience in bank management. Some financial institutions hire undergraduate students to work in their statistical department. These individuals can gain relevant experience for this career while earning their degree.

Entry-level analysts generally need to complete an apprenticeship program in which they learn about investment analysis and other financial functions before they can work independently in this field. Trainees typically gain increased responsibility as they acquire experience.

Some Investment Analysts choose to pursue the designation of Chartered Financial Analyst (CFA) after they gain some experience in this field. This designation is generally recognized in the industry as a mark of professional excellence. Candidates need to pass a series of three examinations over a period of three years and have three years of work experience to earn this distinction.

Finances Required Before Earning

Individuals who are interested in this career should budget for the costs of postsecondary education. At public home-state universities, undergraduate tuition frequently costs between $6,000 and $16,000 per year. Students from out of state may pay additional fees. Private colleges often charge from $15,000 to more than $30,000 annually for undergraduate tuition. Graduate students usually pay about the same as or slightly more than undergraduate students for tuition. Individuals should also budget for living expenses, which frequently range from $5,000 to $15,000 annually. Books and supplies may cost about $1,000 each year.

Financial Aid Information

For a free booklet on financial aid, one may write to or e-mail the following:
Financial Aids for Students
Finney Company
3943 Meadowbrook Road
Minneapolis, Minnesota 55426-4505
feedback@finney-hobar.com

Attractive Features

Many Investment Analysts find their work interesting. They may appreciate the variety and challenges that accompany this career. Individuals in this profession may have opportunities to travel to many different locations and interact with a broad variety of people. They may gain a sense of satisfaction when companies' projects that they helped promote are successful.

Disadvantages

Investment Analysts regularly need to make decisions and take risks involving large amounts of money. If an investment does not succeed, they may cost their employer and many investors a great deal of money. These professionals may feel frustrated if a project fails because of factors, such as fluctuations in the securities market and changes in economic trends, over which they have no control.

Analysts may find their work physically and emotionally tiring at times. They typically work sixty or more hours a week and may frequently need to travel to different locations. Some professionals in this field find that their work schedule is disruptive to their personal life. This position often involves a high level of stress, which can cause health problems for analysts if they are unable to manage the stress.

Outlook for the Future

Employment experts predict that the job market for Investment Analysts in the United States should remain strong through the year 2015. Factors such as globalization of securities markets, deregulation of the financial industry, and growth in mutual funds will likely contribute to the positive outlook for this career. The number of new employment opportunities for analysts typically fluctuates with changes in the economy, however. Many investors decrease their investments during economic downturns. Candidates for a position in this field will likely face a high level of competition. Individuals who have an advanced degree and some investment experience should have an advantage over other applicants in securing a job as an Investment Analyst.

Licensing, Unions, Organizations

Some Investment Analysts choose to obtain the designation of Chartered Financial Analyst (CFA), which the CFA Institute offers. In addition, individuals in this profession may need to obtain a securities license from the National Association of Securities Dealers (NASD). They can also choose to become members of the NASD.

Suggested Courses in High School

Students who are interested in this career should take college-preparatory courses, including classes in English, mathematics, science, social studies, and a foreign language. They should also take accounting, economics, business, and other finance-related courses in high school. In addition, these individuals can benefit from enrolling in computer and information science classes.

Suggested High School Activities

Prospective Investment Analysts can improve their communication skills by participating in debate and drama groups. They can gain knowledge of business procedures by joining a business club. Students may also be able to gain applicable experience for this career by working part-time or during the summer in a bank, brokerage house, or stock exchange. They can read about the stock market and other finance-related topics in newspapers, in financial publications, and on the Internet.

Methods to Enter Work

Individuals who are interested in this career can apply for an entry-level finance or statistical position at large commercial banks, brokerage houses, and the investment departments of insurance companies. As they gain experience and make employment contacts, they may have opportunities to advance to the position of Investment Analyst. Individuals may also be able to make employment contacts by completing an internship program while they obtain their bachelor's or master's degree.

Candidates may be able to learn about employment opportunities by contacting the placement office of the college or university from which they graduated. They can also contact state or private employment agencies. Employers may advertise available positions in the classified sections of newspapers or on the Internet. In addition, applicants can apply directly to companies for which they would like to work.

Additional Information

American Academy of Financial Management
102 Beverly Drive
Metairie, Louisiana 70001
http://www.financialanalyst.org

CFA Institute
560 Ray C. Hunt Drive
Charlottesville, Virginia 22903
http://www.cfainstitute.org

Financial Planning Association
4100 East Mississippi Avenue, Suite 400
Denver, Colorado 80246-3053
http://www.fpanet.org

Related Web Sites

Investment FAQ
http://invest-faq.com
This Web site offers information about investing and personal finance, stocks, bonds, discount brokers, informational resources, retirement plans, and life insurance.

Investopedia.com
http://www.investopedia.com
Viewers of this Web site can learn about investments and access tutorials, a dictionary of investing terms, and additional resources.

Testing Your Interests

How can you know if you are suited to this occupation? Ask yourself these questions. If you answer "yes" to most of them and the job sounds interesting, you may want to look into this vocation further as a possible career.

1. Am I interested in economics and finance?

2. Can I work well with many different people?

3. Do I enjoy challenges and work well under pressure?

4. Am I honest, and do I have a strong sense of ethics?

5. Do I have good judgment and analytical skills?

6. Am I comfortable making decisions and taking responsibility for them?

Published by Finney Company, Minneapolis, Minnesota 55426-4505
© Finney Company 2005

Occupational Guidance

Foreign Service Management Officer

Description of Work

The U.S. Department of State employs Foreign Service officers to work in more than 250 diplomatic and consular posts throughout the world. Professionals in this field are also stationed in Washington, DC, and at regional sites, such as in Miami, Florida, in the continental United States.

Individuals in this profession help establish and maintain friendly relations with the governments of foreign countries. They also keep the U.S. government informed about developments in the political, social, and economic conditions of foreign countries. The U.S. Secretary of State relies on Foreign Service officers' reports in making policy decisions, and these professionals in turn help enforce the department's policy decisions. In addition, officers are responsible for extending protection to American citizens abroad.

Foreign Service officers may specialize in one of five functional areas, or *cones*, which include management, consular, economic, political, and public diplomacy functions. Regardless of their specialty area, these professionals serve as representatives of the United States. Their actions during and outside of work hours reflect on the U.S. government. As a result, individuals need to pass an intensive security check before they can begin working in this position.

Individuals who specialize in a management cone are known as Foreign Service Management Officers. They typically have some prior training, education, or other management experience. These specialists may have a background in areas ranging from real estate or building maintenance to human resources or construction management. They usually receive additional training regarding their particular post once they enter a Foreign Service position.

During training, officers may learn about administrative practices, leadership skills, budget applications, supervisory training, and general services operations. General services operations typically include the management of in-house operations, such as leasing residences for personnel, the operation and acquisition of vehicles for embassy use, or the maintenance of embassy facilities and staff residences, as well as the management and supervision of general services operation personnel. In addition, officers may need to learn a specified foreign language before they assume a post.

After they have completed the training period, Foreign Service Management Officers are typically assigned to an overseas post. They may not be able to choose their post. Instead, these individuals need to be willing to handle assignments in locations around the world. The U.S. government generally pays for their travel and living expenses.

Regardless of their particular post, officers usually perform duties that are similar to those they would perform if they were stationed in the United States. The size of the staff at an overseas post is often smaller than the staff in a U.S. office, however. Therefore, overseas offices may have less division of labor than U.S. offices. Individuals stationed in international posts may need to handle a wide variety of duties.

Foreign Service Management Officers work under the direction of the ambassador or deputy chief ambassador. They need to be prepared to handle many different types of job duties. Depending on their post and their training and experience, officers' responsibilities may include American citizen services, foreign real estate affairs, human resource management, agency relations, or the direction of visits from members of Congress. These professionals generally work to achieve foreign policy objectives, direct the preparation of budget submissions, and oversee the staffing and management of post personnel.

Depending on the level of security in a specific country, the U.S. Department of State may encourage its employees to take advantage of opportunities to interact with people in the community in which they live. Officers typically have comfortable living quarters that meet American standards of sanitation. If there are no available government-owned

GOE 11.09.03/O*Net 19005A
O*Net-Soc 11-1011.01

living accommodations, the Department of State tries to provide quarters that conform to American standards for these professionals.

In some posts, the U.S. Embassy may provide a commissary that imports duty-free items for resale to American staff members. In most locations, however, individuals in this profession can purchase most of the items they need through the local economy. The Department of State may provide access to foods popular in the United States so Foreign Service staff members do not entirely need to adjust to a new diet. Many officers choose to experience the differences in food, customs, and climate in their assigned country, however.

Individuals who want to learn more about Foreign Service employment opportunities may want to read about the occupation of Foreign Service Officer (*Occupational Guidance* Vol. III, Unit 5H, No. 16). People who want to learn about other careers related to this profession can read about the occupations of Human Resources Manager (*Occupational Guidance* Vol. II, Unit 4H, No. 14), Chamber of Commerce Manager (Vol. VII, Unit 3H, No. 8), and Office Manager (Vol. III, Unit 1I, No. 14).

Earnings

Foreign Service Management Officers' salaries vary according to their service rating or grade. Although the Foreign Service is a part of the federal government, the service has a different set of employment regulations than the civil service or the military.

The Foreign Service typically considers officers' levels of education and experience when determining their salary. The starting salary for individuals in this profession often ranges between $35,000 and $63,000 a year. Highly experienced Foreign Service Management Officers may earn around $140,000 annually.

Individuals in this profession typically receive comprehensive benefits in addition to their salary. The federal government may provide paid vacation time and sick leave, life and health insurance, and a pension plan. The U.S. Department of State pays for the moving expenses for officers who are assigned to an overseas post. Individuals who are stationed in some countries may receive additional compensation to offset high costs of living, hardship, or hazardous duties. The government may also compensate professionals for some of the expenses associated with their children's education.

History of Occupation

Prior to adopting the Constitution in 1787, the United States had representatives stationed abroad to perform the functions of consuls. Benjamin Franklin, Thomas Jefferson, and John Quincy Adams were all emissaries and diplomats before and after the United States obtained its independence. The U.S. Congress created the consular service in 1792. According to the Constitution, the President of the United States was responsible for appointing consuls, subject to the approval of the Senate. The government often appointed business leaders who were living abroad to a consular office. The majority of these professionals did not receive salaries for their work as a consul, but they were permitted to keep any fees they collected for performing official services. In 1855, the U.S. Congress passed a law that established a regular consular system. This law provided for salaries for consuls and prohibited the consuls from participating in private business activities.

The Rogers Act of 1924 combined the consular and diplomatic services into the single organization of the Foreign Service of the United States. This Act also standardized officers' salaries and provided for an advancement system based on merit. It also accomplished other reforms in the Foreign Service system.

The Foreign Service Act of 1946 replaced the Rogers Act of 1924. This legislation helped restore the overseas functions of the U.S. Department of State. In addition, the act increased the strength of the administrative structure of the department.

Present-day Foreign Service Management Officers work to promote the image of the United States abroad. They also protect American citizens who are traveling internationally or who live abroad and help provide economic and other aid to developing or struggling nations.

Working Conditions

Foreign Service Management Officers frequently interact with other people throughout their workday. These professionals typically have a clean, comfortable, and well-equipped office. Depending on the size of the Foreign Service staff, officers may work independently to complete some projects. They generally need to report to a supervisory official, however.

Hours of Work

Foreign Service Management Officers usually work at least forty hours a week, Monday through Friday. They may frequently need to work overtime, however, particularly during visits of U.S. officials, if they attend hosted events, or if they work in an unstable political climate.

Ability Required

Individuals in this profession need to have excellent verbal and written communication skills. They often supervise local staff members. Therefore, they should also have good leadership and problem-solving skills. Officers should have an aptitude for working with numbers and financial information, including budgets. They need to be able to plan their activities and schedules and set priories. Professionals in this field should be skilled in using different types of computer technology. In addition, they need to be healthy and in good physical condition.

Temperament Required

Foreign Service Management Officers serve as representatives of the United States. Therefore, they need to have a high standard of ethics and be continuously aware of the image they project. Officers need to be flexible and willing to adjust to changes in their schedule. They should handle stress and pressure well. In addition, professionals in this field need to adjust well to living in foreign countries.

Education and Training Required

Foreign Service Management Officers typically need to have a minimum of a high school diploma or the equivalent. The U.S. Department of State often prefers to hire candidates who have a bachelor's or graduate-level degree for a position as a Foreign Service Management Officer, however.

Prospective Foreign Service officers who choose to pursue postsecondary education often major in an area of the liberal arts. They may also obtain a degree in an area such as public administration. In addition, these individuals can benefit from taking business-related courses.

Applicants for a position as a Foreign Service officer need to be between the ages of twenty and fifty-nine. They also need to be a citizen of the United States and be willing to accept an assignment at a post anywhere in the world, including Washington, DC. As part of the application process, they need to pass written and oral competitive examinations, extensive security checks, and physical examinations. In addition, these individuals may need to learn a foreign language. Once they join the Foreign Service, they may complete from three months to one year of training.

After they have completed two initial tours of service, Foreign Service Management Officers may be appointed to a post for a period ranging from twelve months to three years. The Foreign Service may then transfer or assign them to another post.

Finances Required Before Earning

Most individuals who are interested in this career choose to pursue a postsecondary degree. They should budget for the associated educational expenses. At public home-state universities, undergraduate tuition often costs between $6,000 and $16,000 each year. Students from out of state may pay additional fees. Private colleges may charge from $15,000 to more than $30,000 annually for undergraduate tuition. Graduate students typically pay about the same as or slightly more than undergraduate students for tuition. Individuals should also budget for living expenses, which frequently range from $5,000 to $15,000 annually. Books and supplies may cost about $1,000 per year.

Financial Aid Information

For a free booklet on financial aid, one may write to or e-mail the following:

Financial Aids for Students
Finney Company
3943 Meadowbrook Road
Minneapolis, Minnesota 55426-4505
feedback@finney-hobar.com

Attractive Features

People may be attracted to this career by the opportunities to experience other cultures and travel to international locations. Foreign Service Management Officers meet many different people in their work. They often appreciate the challenges and variety of tasks that accompany this career. They may gain a sense of satisfaction in helping to maintain international relations for the United States government.

Disadvantages

Foreign Service officers typically cannot choose the location of their post. Therefore, they may feel disappointed if they are stationed in a country that they would not have chosen. Some people in this profession have difficulty adjusting to a new culture, climate, or foods. They often spend several years at a post and may have few opportunities to visit their family or friends who are located in the United States. Officers may be in physical danger if the political climate of the country in which they are stationed is unstable or if the country has tense relations with the United States.

Outlook for the Future

The number of new employment opportunities for Foreign Service Management Officers will likely vary according to the state of world affairs and increases or decreases in government funding for the Foreign Service. Candidates may find job openings as current officers are promoted to top department management positions, transfer to other occupations, or retire from the service. Individuals who achieve high scores on examinations and who pass medical and security clearances are typically given priority over other applicants in the hiring process.

Licensing, Unions, Organizations

Individuals in this profession can choose to join a professional organization, such as the American Federation of Government Employees and the National Federation of Federal Employees. Many of these individuals also become members of the American Foreign Service Association.

Suggested Courses in High School

Students who plan to pursue postsecondary education should take college-preparatory courses, including classes in English, mathematics, science, social studies, and a foreign language. Individuals who are interested in this career can also benefit from taking courses in business, computer science, and bookkeeping.

Suggested High School Activities

Prospective Foreign Service Management Officers can learn about current events and international affairs through news media and publications. They can gain experience working with different people by volunteering with community organizations. Students can improve their communication and interpersonal skills by participating in a variety of extracurricular activities, such as speech, drama, debate, student council, or team athletic activities. In addition, they can gain experience living away from home and adjusting to new surroundings by attending a summer camp.

Methods to Enter Work

Individuals who are interested in this career can begin the application process by taking the Foreign Service Written Examination. There are hundreds of testing centers worldwide that administer this examination annually in April. Candidates who pass the test may be invited to attend an all-day oral assessment. People can learn about the examination and assessment processes and read about the Diplomats in Residence program available at numerous universities throughout the United States by visiting the following Web site: http://www.careers.state.gov

Once individuals pass all the necessary examinations, including a medical and security clearance, their name is placed on a list. They may then be called to enter a class. If their name remains on the list for more than eighteen months, however, their candidacy typically expires.

Additional Information

American Foreign Service Association
2101 E Street NW
Washington, DC 20037
http://www.afsa.org

Office of Recruitment, Examination and Employment
U.S. Department of State
2401 E Street NW, Suite 518 H
Washington, DC 20522
http://www.state.gov/m/dghr/hr/

Related Web Sites

Associates of the American Foreign Service Worldwide
http://www.aafsw.org
This Web site features information about a variety of topics, including living in Washington, DC, and living abroad. Viewers can also access links to related resources.

Transitions Abroad
http://www.transitionsabroad.com
Visitors to this Web site can learn about working, studying, living, or traveling abroad.

U.S. Department of State: Travel and Living Abroad
http://www.state.gov/travel
This resource provides updates for and educates travelers and individuals living abroad. Viewers can find information about emergencies and warnings, passports, and visas. They can also access links to related resources, including the Web site for the Centers for Disease Control and resources that offer information about exchange rates, U.S. customs, and aviation safety data.

Testing Your Interests

How can you know if you are suited to this occupation? Ask yourself these questions. If you answer "yes" to most of them and the job sounds interesting, you may want to look into this vocation further as a possible career.

1. Do I enjoy traveling, and am I interested in other cultures?

2. Do I have a strong sense of ethics and personal integrity?

3. Can I adapt well to new situations and environments?

4. Do I enjoy working with many different people?

5. Can I remain aware of the image I am projecting and serve as a positive representative of the United States?

Published by Finney Company, Minneapolis, Minnesota 55426-4505
© Finney Company 2005

Occupational Guidance

Employment Recruiter

Description of Work

Many companies and organizations staff a human resources department to recruit, screen, interview, and refer prospective employees. Employment Recruiters are typically members of the human resources team. They help their employing company or organization match available positions to the applicants most suited for the positions.

The policies of a company or organization may affect the specific procedures recruiters follow. Some employers have a receptionist or another employee supervise the application process; in other offices, a recruiter may be responsible for this task. Some large human resources departments divide the interviewing duties among the staff members, who may specialize in performing certain tasks. Most companies and organizations assign one person to work with potential employees throughout the application and placement processes, however. This system allows the Employment Recruiter to talk with and thoroughly evaluate prospective employees.

Many employers require applicants to take examinations, such as computer or typing tests, to determine the individuals' skill levels in completing certain types of tasks. Employment Recruiters are usually responsible for administering the tests. They may choose from a variety of examination options and select the ones that are most appropriate for the available position. These professionals then score the tests and evaluate the results.

In order to accurately assess prospective employees' aptitude for a position, Employment Recruiters need to be familiar with the duties involved in the position. They should understand what types of education, experience, and other qualifications candidates need to have. These professionals should also be able to discuss factors such as wages, working conditions, and opportunities for advancement with applicants. Recruiters may learn about the different positions within a company or organization by discussing the positions with the supervisors of other departments. In addition, some employers provide standard job descriptions

for various positions. The human resources department may maintain these descriptions.

Recruiters are responsible for finding people to fill jobs. They may use a variety of methods, depending on the procedures their employing company or organization approves, to search for candidates. For example, these professionals may list available positions in the classified sections of newspapers, on the Internet, or through state or private employment agencies. They may also contact employment agencies to review posted résumés of people searching for similar positions. In addition, recruiters may contact the placement offices of career and technical schools, community colleges, or four-year colleges and universities to inquire about graduates who may be suited for the position. They sometimes visit college campuses or attend job fairs, professional association meetings, or community events in order to interview potential employees.

When a prospective employee comes to the office of a company or organization, Employment Recruiters may ask the individual to complete an application form, regardless of whether the applicant has previously submitted a résumé. Many employers prefer to have formal applications on file for candidates. Recruiters may clarify or explain some sections of the application form or ask the candidate for additional information.

If they feel an applicant may be suited for the position, recruiters typically schedule an interview. During the interview, they need to closely observe the applicant and attempt to determine the individual's personality and abilities. These professionals can often gain insight into an individual's character by asking the candidate about personal hobbies, interests, and former employment experience. They usually discuss the position, including the duties involved in the job, any special requirements of the position, and the general working conditions, with the interviewee. If recruiters think the applicant is qualified for the job, they may elaborate on factors such as the rate of pay, the specific work schedule, and company policies.

Employment Recruiters may then arrange an interview between the applicant and the supervisor or manager of

GOE 11.03.04/O*Net 21511E
O*Net-Soc 13-1071.02

the open position. If the manager approves the applicant, recruiters are often responsible for handling the final details of arranging employment. These professionals may also send notices to other candidates who had applied for the position to let them know the position has been filled and to thank them for applying.

In most companies, the human resources office maintains permanent records of applications, test results, and other information for people employed at the company. Recruiters may also keep on file applications of people whom the company may consider for future employment opportunities. In addition, some companies maintain information about candidates who are available for part-time or short-term jobs. If an employer needs to hire a part-time or temporary employee, recruiters may check their files and contact people until they find the right candidate for the position.

A few months after an individual is hired, Employment Recruiters may conduct another interview to determine whether the employee is happy with the position and if the individual is performing the work satisfactorily. Before the interview, recruiters may consult with the employee's supervisor. They may also check an evaluation or rating of the employee if one is available. If they identify any problems, these professionals may address the issues during the interview.

In addition to being involved in the hiring process, Employment Recruiters may be responsible for conducting an exit interview when an employee leaves the company. These professionals try to determine the actual reasons the individual is departing and learn whether the employee has any grievances against the supervisor, coworkers, department, or company. If a department has an unusually high turnover rate for employees, recruiters may rely on exit interviews to identify the reasons for the turnover. Some firms conduct periodic analyses of employee turnover. Individuals who work for such companies may ask departing employees to complete an evaluation form, which the company may later use to compile and analyze data regarding turnover.

Individuals who are interested in this career may also want to read about other human resources occupations, including Compensation Manager (*Occupational Guidance* Vol. V, Unit 2I, No. 1), Organization Development Specialist (Vol. II, Unit 1I, No. 3), Human Resources Manager (Vol. II, Unit 4H, No. 14), and Labor Relations Specialist (Vol. VI, Unit 1I, No. 20).

Earnings

The annual earnings for human resources professionals vary according to the individuals' level of education and experience and their employing organization's size, economic activity, and geographic location. Entry-level recruiters with a bachelor's degree often earn from about $30,000 to $39,000 annually. The starting salary for individuals with an advanced degree is often higher than for employees with a bachelor's degree. As they gain experience, recruiters' salaries may range from $40,000 to $54,000 annually. Individuals in an executive position who have many years of experience may earn $74,000 or more per year.

Most employers offer benefits to full-time staff members of their human resources department. Employment Recruiters often receive health insurance; paid sick leave, holidays, and vacation time; and retirement benefits.

History of Occupation

Prior to the 20th century, most employers did not staff a human resources department or establish standard hiring procedures. Instead, they often personally made decisions about whether to hire an applicant based on the individual's personality, appearance, or other traits. Some employers had difficulty judging the character and aptitude of candidates and often experienced high employee turnover rates.

As businesses and industrial organizations expanded and became increasingly specialized, many employers began to recognize the need to improve their labor-management relations and employed human resources professionals to address the problems. During the early part of the 20th century, some people started to study scientific management and industrial psychology. Frank Gilbreth, an American engineer and building contractor, developed a time-and-motion study. He conducted the research in an effort to achieve scientific management and improvement in his company.

Around this time, some psychologists began to focus on applying the science of psychology to industrial settings. Hugo Munsterberg published the book *Psychology and Industrial Efficiency*, which led to other studies in the field.

After World War I, many businesses and industrial organizations changed their methods of hiring and managing employees. The work of human resources professionals became more technical and complex than it had previously been. Many employers started to require candidates for available positions to complete various tests and personal interviews.

Most present-day companies continue to establish and use standardized hiring practices. They rely on Employment Recruiters to handle many of the processes involved in finding and hiring personnel.

Working Conditions

Employment Recruiters typically have a comfortable office space. They may work for industrial firms, businesses, government agencies, and other types of organizations. They typically have a desk and computer in their office and have access to various types of company records and files. Many companies and organizations maintain electronic personnel records on a computer. Large offices may employ numerous human resources professionals, while the personnel department of small offices may consist of one person.

Employment Recruiters may communicate with a variety of people in person, via e-mail, and over the telephone throughout their workday. They may need to administer many different tests for some positions, while they may only need to interview candidates for other positions. Professionals in this field may also spend some time observing employees while at work. In addition, they may spend time traveling to meetings and other engagements, such as job fairs, outside the office.

Hours of Work

The standard workweek for most Employment Recruiters ranges from thirty-five to forty hours. These individuals may occasionally need to work overtime, however. They may travel in the evenings or on weekends if they need to go to other cities.

Ability Required

Employment Recruiters should have excellent listening, communication, and interpersonal skills. They need to be able to work with many different types of people. These individuals should also be accurate judges of other people's character and personality.

Professionals in this field need to be knowledgeable about their employing company's operations and the different positions within the company. They should have a good memory, especially for information regarding labor laws, equal employment opportunity (EEO) guidelines, affirmative action laws, regulations pertaining to the Americans with Disabilities Act, and safety and health issues.

Recruiters need to have excellent organizational skills. They may need to maintain many different types of records. These professionals should be able to perform a variety of tasks, particularly if they work for a small company. They should have computer skills and be familiar with several different computer programs.

Temperament Required

Employment Recruiters should enjoy working with many different types of people. They should be resourceful and be willing to take initiative when seeking information about a candidate's previous employment experience or the reason a current employee wants to leave the company. Recruiters should be accurate, thorough, and detail-oriented in their work. They need to handle pressure well. In addition, these professionals should be emotionally stable and mature and be tactful, patient, and understanding in their interactions with others.

Education and Training Required

Most companies and organizations require candidates to have a minimum of a bachelor's degree to qualify for a position as an Employment Recruiter, and they may prefer to hire applicants with a graduate degree in human resources or business administration. Individuals who are interested in this career often major in business, personnel administration, human resources management, or labor or industrial

relations. They also typically take courses in English, psychology, speech, and statistics. In addition, some employers require candidates to have specialized knowledge in a particular field of industry or business.

Once individuals secure a position as an Employment Recruiter, they may receive on-the-job training. Entry-level professionals often work with and observe experienced recruiters for several weeks or months until they become familiar with the different functions of the job. Some companies prefer to promote people who have worked in other human resources jobs to the position of recruiter.

Finances Required Before Earning

Individuals who are interested in this career should budget for the costs of postsecondary education. At public home-state universities, undergraduate tuition often costs from $6,000 to $16,000 per year. Students from out of state may pay additional fees. Private colleges may charge from $15,000 to more than $30,000 per year for undergraduate tuition. Graduate school tuition usually costs about the same as or slightly more than undergraduate tuition. Students should also budget for living expenses, which frequently range from $5,000 to $15,000 annually. Books and supplies may cost about $1,000 per year.

Financial Aid Information

For a free booklet on financial aid, one may write to or e-mail the following:

Financial Aids for Students
Finney Company
3943 Meadowbrook Road
Minneapolis, Minnesota 55426-4505
feedback@finney-hobar.com

Attractive Features

Employment Recruiters may appreciate the daily challenges, variety of tasks, and opportunities to work with different people that accompany this career. They may gain a sense of satisfaction when they fill a position with a candidate who is well suited to the work. Individuals in this profession typically have a high level of job security. In addition, they may find opportunities for advancement.

Disadvantages

Employment Recruiters may dislike dismissing candidates who are not suited for a particular position. They may sometimes have difficulty choosing between two qualified applicants. In addition, these professionals may dislike conducting exit interviews if employees are angry or resentful toward the company. Some people find the routine testing and other detail tasks involved in this career to be tedious. Individuals who dislike working with others may not be suited for this profession.

Outlook for the Future

The job market for Employment Recruiters will likely remain strong through the year 2012. Many companies and organizations rely on recruiters to manage the hiring processes and other personnel concerns. There are many qualified candidates for this position, however. Therefore, applicants will likely face strong competition for available jobs. Individuals may find position openings as people currently working in the field are promoted, transfer to other occupations, or retire from the workforce. They may also find increasing numbers of job opportunities in the specialty areas of diversity or international human resources. Candidates who have prior experience working in another human resources position and those who have an advanced degree may have an advantage over other applicants in securing a job as an Employment Recruiter.

Licensing, Unions, Organizations

Employment Recruiters are not typically union members. Many individuals in this profession choose to join professional organizations, however, such as the Society for Human Resource Management, the International Public Management Association for Human Resources, or the the National Human Resources Association.

In most government agencies, this position is part of the civil-service program. Therefore, applicants for government recruiting jobs may need to take a civil-service examination.

Some professionals in this field choose to become certified. The Human Resource Certification Institute, which is part of the Society for Human Resource Management, offers a certification program.

Suggested Courses in High School

Students who are interested in a career as an Employment Recruiter should take courses in English, speech, and psychology in high school. Through these classes, they can improve their communication skills and learn about human interactions. Individuals can learn about business and management through social studies, economics, business, and current affairs classes. They can improve their attention to detail and their aptitude for working with numbers and statistics by enrolling in mathematics classes. In addition, students who want to pursue this career can benefit from taking computer classes and any remaining college-preparatory courses.

Suggested High School Activities

Prospective Employment Recruiters can improve their interpersonal and communication skills by participating in a variety of extracurricular activities, including drama, debate, student council, and team athletic activities. They can gain experience working with a variety of people by volunteering with different community organizations and programs. Individuals may also be able to gain applicable experience for this career by working part-time or during the summer in an office.

Methods to Enter Work

Graduates of a college or university can contact their school's placement office for assistance in finding employment in this field. Companies may also advertise openings in their human resources departments through the classified sections of newspapers, on the Internet, or through state or private employment agencies. Individuals can also directly contact companies, organizations, and agencies for which they would like to work to inquire about available positions and application requirements.

Additional Information

American Society for Training & Development
1640 King Street, Box 1443
Alexandria, Virginia 22313-2043
http://www.astd.org

Society for Human Resource Management
1800 Duke Street
Alexandria, Virginia 22314
http://www.shrm.org

Related Web Sites

About: Human Resources
http://humanresources.about.com
Viewers of this Web site can find articles and links to additional resources about human resources management.

Workforce Management
http://www.workforce.com
This Web site features information about labor management and human resources topics, including compensation and benefits, legal issues, recruiting and staffing, training and development, computer software, and other technology.

Testing Your Interests

How can you know if you are suited to this occupation? Ask yourself these questions. If you answer "yes" to most of them and the job sounds interesting, you may want to look into this vocation further as a possible career.

1. Do I enjoy working with a variety of people?

2. Am I a good judge of character?

3. Am I thorough, accurate, and detail-oriented in my work?

4. Do I have strong listening, communication, and interpersonal skills?

Published by Finney Company, Minneapolis, Minnesota 55426-4505

Occupational Guidance

Housekeeper-Companion

Description of Work

Some people do not have the time or physical abilities to perform many daily tasks and chores. These individuals may choose to hire a Housekeeper-Companion to perform such tasks and to provide them with company. Housekeeper-Companions may also be known as live-ins, maids, caregivers, housekeepers, home-care attendants, companions, or nannies.

Housekeeper-Companions regulate their work according to the needs of the household in which they are employed. Their tasks may vary according to the particular circumstances of the people who rely on their services. For example, an individual who works for a family with school-age children may maintain the employer's house during the day and then serve as a companion to the children in the late afternoons and evenings. Another Housekeeper-Companion may care for a person who is disabled, elderly, ill, or needs special attention for other reasons. A third individual in this profession may work for a single person who is employed full-time and does not want to live alone. The housekeeper helps the employer complete the domestic chores involved in maintaining a home. In addition, some people employ a couple of individuals, rather than a single Housekeeper-Companion, to serve in one or more of these capacities.

In their role as a housekeeper, individuals in this profession are generally responsible for managing a home under their employer's direction. In some cases, these employees may be completely responsible for making decisions when problems arise concerning the house. Employers typically outline the scope of the household duties when they hire Housekeeper-Companions.

Housekeepers are also usually responsible for planning menus, preparing meals, and shopping for groceries and household supplies. They may have the freedom to select the food, beverages, and other household goods they prefer, or they may follow the directions of their employer. If a resident of the home needs to observe a special diet, these employees consider the individual's diet when planning meals and shopping and cooking food. They should prepare well-balanced and nutritious meals. Housekeepers usually try to offer a variety of menus. They may need to keep accurate records of their purchases.

In some homes, housekeepers may be in charge of decorating or maintaining the house or apartment, particularly if there are no other domestic employees. To perform this function, they may choose or clean furniture, floors, carpeting, windows, and other items. They may also hang seasonal decorations. If the employer hires other domestic employees, however, housekeepers may delegate such tasks to the assistants and supervise their work. They may also be responsible for interviewing prospective domestic employees, hiring or discharging the individuals, and paying them for their work.

In their role as a companion, individuals in this profession may perform more varied duties than are involved in the housekeeping aspect of this career. Their specific tasks vary according to the needs of their employer. Companions may need practical nursing skills to care for some residents of a home. They are not usually a trained nurse, however. Therefore, they do not need to fulfill all the functions of these medical professionals. Instead, companions often administer medications under a physician's instructions or assist individuals with therapeutic exercises. These employees may also supervise the activities of children in a family, though such work is not usually one of their primary duties.

Some people who have difficulty reading or are unable to read rely on companions to read to them. Companions may accompany their employer on shopping trips, to meetings, or on other outings. The main duty of these employees is to be available to assist their employer when necessary. They may sit and talk with the individual at times, answer the telephone, and perform other duties.

GOE 10.03.03/O*Net 62061
O*Net-Soc 39-9021.00

Some individuals in this profession travel with their employer. They may travel to locations throughout the country or abroad if their employer takes such trips. While they travel, these individuals typically serve primarily as a companion, rather than as a housekeeper. They usually perform housekeeping duties if necessary at the places where they stay. In addition, these employees may be responsible for making travel arrangements and handling various details involved in each move.

Individuals who are interested in this career may also want to read about related occupations, including Licensed Practical Nurse (*Occupational Guidance* Vol. IV, Unit 2I, No. 19), Child-Care Provider (Vol. VI, Unit 1I, No. 9), Residential Adviser (Vol. VIII, Unit 2I, No. 5), Housekeeper (Hotel/Motel) (Vol. I, Unit 4H, No. 3), and Hospital Executive Housekeeper (Vol. VI, Unit 2I, No. 10).

Earnings

Housekeeper-Companions typically earn from about $13,000 to $25,000 per year. Their incomes may vary according to several factors, including the number of hours they work. The average annual income for individuals in this profession is about $17,000. Housekeeper-Companions who have specialized skills and experience may earn significantly more than other people in this field, however. These individuals often earn from $1,000 to more than $1,500 per week, or from about $52,000 to more than $78,000 annually for full-time employees. Housekeeper-Companions typically negotiate for their wages or other types of compensation, such as paid travel expenses or seasonal bonuses.

Live-in companions usually receive room and board in addition to their earnings. Some employers also offer benefits, such as paid holidays and vacation time, health and life insurance, and retirement plans, for full-time employees.

History of Occupation

Some people in ancient cultures probably performed the work of Housekeeper-Companions. The first people to serve in this function may have been slaves of royalty and nobles of ancient kingdoms.

In many later cultures, women of nobility status often employed ladies-in-waiting. These individuals served as companions for their employer and attended to various personal duties. Ladies-in-waiting did not typically perform housekeeping tasks, however. Their employer typically hired other staff members to perform such work.

During the 18th and 19th centuries, many families in various cultures maintained full staffs of household employees. Some families, particularly if they included an elderly person or someone who was incapacitated in some way, also hired an individual to act as a companion.

During the 20th century in the United States, many people who needed special assistance or companionship began to hire individuals to fulfill the combined functions of both housekeepers and companions. The specific duties these employees performed varied according to the individual needs of their employer. Present-day Housekeeper-Companions continue to assist people with domestic tasks, including cleaning, grocery shopping, and meal preparation, while providing companionship for their employer.

Working Conditions

The working conditions for Housekeeper-Companions vary according to the specific position in which they work. These individuals typically work in private homes. As housekeepers, they may personally do laundry, iron clothes, wash dishes, mop floors, vacuum, and perform other tasks, or they may supervise other employees who complete the tasks. Some homes have many different appliances, such as a dishwasher, while other homes have few such devices. Individuals in this profession may travel to different locations throughout the community, including grocery stores, pharmacies, and other facilities.

In their role as companions, these individuals may travel to different cities or countries with their employer. They may perform a range of duties, including caring for someone who is ill, reading to their employer, bringing food or drinks to someone who is immobile, or playing cards or other games with their employer. Individuals in this profession often live on-site at their employer's residence.

Hours of Work

Housekeeper-Companions are typically full-time employees. They may work about forty hours a week. Individuals who live at their employer's residence may work additional hours, however. They may handle household tasks during the day and spend time with their employer or other residents of the household in the evenings. Individuals who do not live on-site often have leisure time in the evenings. Regardless of where they live, Housekeeper-Companions typically have at least one day and one evening off each week. They may have a standard day off, or the day may change each week.

Ability Required

Housekeeper-Companions should be skilled in performing various household tasks, including cooking, cleaning, and basic home maintenance duties. They should understand how to use most home appliances. These individuals should also be knowledgeable about nutrition. In addition, they should be able to administer first aid and perform some home nursing tasks.

Housekeeper-Companions should have strong communication and interpersonal skills. They need to be able to make others feel comfortable. In addition, they should have good telephone etiquette and practice appropriate social behaviors in different types of situations.

Temperament Required

Housekeeper-Companions should present a calm, stable, and patient demeanor. They should work well with a variety of people. These individuals should be tactful, honest, and discreet in their interactions with their employer and other residents of a home. They should be comfortable handling multiple tasks and making decisions. They should also be comfortable accepting the level of responsibility that accompanies this position.

Education and Training Required

There are no standardized educational requirements for Housekeeper-Companions in the United States. Individuals in this profession may have a broad range of backgrounds and experience. Their specific duties can vary greatly according to the needs of their employer. Some individuals prepare for this career by taking classes in cooking, baking, decorating, nutrition, first aid, home nursing, sewing, or bookkeeping through community education programs, career and technical schools, or community colleges. Some employers prefer to hire an individual who has a bachelor's degree in a particular field, so they can talk with their companion about similar topics they have studied.

Finances Required Before Earning

For many positions in this field, individuals do not need to obtain a postsecondary degree. Instead, they need to have enough money to pay for their living expenses until they receive their first paycheck.

Other prospective Housekeeper-Companions choose to take classes through community education programs, community colleges, career and technical schools, or four-year colleges or universities. The costs associated with postsecondary education vary according to the type of school individuals attend. Community education programs may charge from $15 to more than $100 per class. At public career and technical schools and community colleges, tuition often costs from $2,000 to $7,000 per year for full-time students. Private career and technical schools may charge from $4,000 to $15,000 annually for tuition. Individuals who attend a public home-state university full-time typically pay between $6,000 and $16,000 a year for tuition. Students from out of state may pay additional fees. At private colleges, tuition often costs from $15,000 to more than $30,000 per year. Students should also budget for living expenses, which frequently range from $5,000 to $15,000 annually. Books and supplies may cost about $1,000 per year.

Financial Aid Information

For a free booklet on financial aid, one may write to or e-mail the following:

Financial Aids for Students
Finney Company
3943 Meadowbrook Road
Minneapolis, Minnesota 55426-4505
feedback@finney-hobar.com

Attractive Features

Individuals who enjoy performing household duties such as decorating, cleaning, and preparing meals may be suited for this career. Housekeeper-Companions have the opportunity to manage a house without the financial burden of maintaining it. Some individuals in this profession live on-site at their employer's residence and receive free room and board. They may enjoy working closely with their employer and the other people who live in the home. Depending on their particular employer, individuals in this profession may have opportunities to travel.

Disadvantages

Housekeeper-Companions who live in their employer's home may rarely have time to themselves. They may become annoyed with their employer or other residents of the home at times because of the close working and living conditions. Individuals in this profession may not have a great deal of flexibility in their schedules. They have to be available to work when their employer needs their assistance.

Outlook for the Future

Experts predict that the number of employment opportunities for Housekeeper-Companions in the United States will likely grow about as fast as the national average through the year 2012. There is a high turnover rate in this field. Therefore, entry-level candidates may find many employment opportunities. People who can provide excellent references, have advanced training, and are willing to clean homes and care for children or adults with special needs may have an advantage over other candidates in securing a position that offers top wages and benefits.

Licensing, Unions, Organizations

Individuals do not need to be licensed to work in this field, though they may choose to pursue certification. Housekeeper-Companions are not typically union members. Some individuals in this profession join organizations that promote their work, such as the National Association for Home Care & Hospice, however.

Suggested Courses in High School

Students who are interested in a career as a Housekeeper-Companion can gain applicable skills by enrolling in family and consumer sciences courses. In these classes, they may learn how to cook, sew, and maintain a house efficiently. Students can improve their communication skills through English and speech courses. They can stay informed about current events and other conversation topics through history and civics classes. Individuals who plan to pursue postsecondary education should take any remaining college-preparatory classes, including courses in mathematics, science, and a foreign language.

Suggested High School Activities

Prospective Housekeeper-Companions can gain applicable experience for this career by completing household tasks in their family's home, working or volunteering in a nursing home or other health-care facility, or babysitting. Through extracurricular activities, including team sports, drama, debate, and student council, students can improve their interpersonal and communication skills.

Methods to Enter Work

Most people who are seeking to hire a Housekeeper-Companion advertise available positions in the classified sections of newspapers. They may also list job openings with state or private employment agencies or on Internet job search Web sites. In addition, candidates may learn about employment opportunities through personal contacts. They should prepare a résumé to present to potential employers.

Additional Information

National Association for Home Care & Hospice
228 Seventh Street SE
Washington, DC 20003
http://www.nahc.org

Related Web Sites

Arbor Hospice & Home Care
http://www.arborhospice.org
This Web site features information about home services, volunteers, jobs in this field, and related resources.

Hospice Association of America
http://www.hospice-america.org
Viewers of this Web site can find information about consumerism, educational opportunities, publications, related products, and links to additional resources.

Testing Your Interests

How can you know if you are suited to this occupation? Ask yourself these questions. If you answer "yes" to most of them and the job sounds interesting, you may want to look into this vocation further as a possible career.

1. Do I enjoy performing household duties?

2. Am I patient and understanding in my interactions with others?

3. Am I physically strong and emotionally stable?

4. Can I work well with a variety of people?

5. Do I enjoy interacting with and helping others?

Published by Finney Company, Minneapolis, Minnesota 55426-4505

Occupational Guidance

School Band Director

Description of Work

Many elementary schools, middle schools, junior and senior high schools, and colleges and universities in the United States offer music courses. Students can study and learn to play instruments through band classes and by participating in extracurricular performance groups. School Band Directors teach band classes and manage the related extracurricular activities.

In some schools, band directors teach other subjects in addition to music classes. Many schools have large enough music programs to allow instructors to concentrate full-time on band- and music-related courses, however. During band classes, directors teach students how to play musical instruments. They may also supervise and conduct the rehearsals and performances of musical groups.

These professionals typically teach regularly scheduled classes during the school day. They often work with a range of students, from beginning-level musicians who are learning to play an instrument to individuals with advanced levels of musical skills. Directors may focus on the techniques of reading music, the processes involved in adapting music to particular instruments, and the techniques of playing harmoniously together. These instructors may also help students understand and overcome problems with their instrument or a piece of music and improve the techniques they use to play their instrument. These professionals typically emphasize the tempo, mood, dynamics, and rhythm of each piece of music. Band directors may work with the entire class at times and with a few students at other times. If one section of the band needs to play a difficult passage, directors often work with the students who are playing the passage until they master it. These teachers also select musicians for solos, duets, or other performances.

Most school bands play for various events during the school year. To prepare for concerts and other performances, directors often schedule extra practice sessions for the band. They typically conduct the rehearsals according to the way they want the students to give the final performance. These professionals work with the musicians to eliminate or resolve any problems. When they prepare for athletic events or parades, nonplaying students such as cheerleaders, drum majors or majorettes, or individuals in the color guard may rehearse and perform with the musicians. Directors may work as closely with these individuals as they do with the band members. For marching bands, the students and director work together to improve the execution of formations.

School Band Directors typically plan the programs for special performances. They may choose the music for students to play at a pep rally or football game. For an annual or semiannual concert, these professionals start planning and training months in advance of the event. They need to choose the music early so the students have as much practice time as possible. Directors sometimes make special arrangements of music or alter the program as they work on the music with their students. They also decide how the band members should enter, sit, group, or leave the performance. These teachers then rehearse the details with the students. Band directors usually prefer to have at least one full-program practice session, or dress rehearsal, at the performance site before each event.

When a group plays in locations outside of the school, directors are usually responsible for making the necessary travel arrangements. They may charter buses to carry students and their instruments or request the use of one of the school's buses for the event. If necessary, these professionals also set up accommodations for overnight stays. They need to follow the school's rules regarding parental permission for trips. During the trip, directors are responsible for supervising the behavior of individual students and the performance of the entire band. In many cases, parents or other adults accompany the group to help supervise the students during the tour.

In addition to conducting classes and preparing for and organizing performances, School Band Directors handle many administrative tasks. They are typically in charge of the band department and are responsible for ordering and maintaining instruments, music, and other equipment. They

GOE 01.04.01/O*Net 34047A
O*Net-Soc 27-2041.01

may make arrangements for necessary repair work and purchase new instruments. These professionals regulate the lending of school instruments to students and make sure the students return the instruments at the end of the academic year.

These teachers are regular faculty members. Therefore, they need to attend faculty meetings, hold conferences with parents, administer tests, grade papers, and submit regular grades for their students.

Band directors are also responsible for maintaining the band rehearsal hall and practice rooms. They supervise the storage of music stands and other equipment and make sure students return the equipment safely to its proper locations. If the school provides uniforms for the band, directors typically supervise the distribution and storage of the uniforms.

School Band Directors may have opportunities to work closely with each of their students. They need to understand the problems these individuals are experiencing. Directors try to gain students' cooperation in practicing faithfully. Students may choose to spend additional hours practicing in the rehearsal room after school. Band teachers may organize extra practice sessions for these students, provide individual lessons, or work with groups of musicians outside of regular class hours.

Individuals who are interested in a career in the educational field may want to read about the occupations of Elementary School Teacher (*Occupational Guidance* Vol. VI, Unit 1I, No. 5) and Secondary School Teacher (Vol. VI, Unit 1I, No. 8). They may also want to read about other music-related careers, such as Choral Director (*Occupational Guidance* Vol. II, Unit 3H, No. 3), Orchestra Leader (Vol. V, Unit 2I, No. 9), Instrumentalist (Vol. V, Unit 5H, No. 7), and Orchestral Musician (Vol. I, Unit 5H, No. 11).

Earnings

School Band Directors' earnings typically vary according to their levels of education and experience, their employer, and their geographic location. The starting salary for band teachers with a bachelor's degree often ranges from about $24,000 to $31,000 a year. For individuals with a master's degree, the starting salary may range between $31,000 and $35,000 a year. As they gain experience, directors' earnings typically increase. Experienced individuals in this profession frequently earn from $40,000 to $56,000 annually. College instructors generally earn more than secondary school teachers. Some directors earn additional income by teaching private music lessons during the evenings and in the summer months.

Most School Band Directors are members of a teacher's union, which negotiates their benefits. These professionals typically receive health insurance, retirement programs, savings plans, and life insurance. They may also receive a mileage allowance, family tuition waivers, and paid sabbatical leaves.

History of Occupation

In the 1850s, the Farm and Trades School of Boston Harbor in Massachusetts established the first school band in the United States. Although historians have found little information about other early American school bands, there were such groups in various parts of the country around the same time. Around 1916, Fred Hanneman organized the first public school band in Richland Center, Wisconsin. As a result of Hanneman's work, other public schools also decided to start bands.

During World War I, most regiments and camps of the armed services had their own band. People in the United States started to develop new interest and enthusiasm for band music. Many schools increased their emphasis on band work and hired qualified teachers to organize and instruct the students. Private manufacturers of instruments sponsored the first national band contest in the 1920s. They held the contest in Chicago, Illinois, and attracted a great deal of attention from musical and educational professionals. Many school personnel felt that schools should not be involved in commercial enterprises, however. In response, the manufacturers asked the National Bureau for the Advancement of Music to sponsor future contests and supplied funds to the organization. The bureau developed state band competitions in addition to the national contest as part of the regular program.

After this point, the number of school bands increased rapidly. Rural and urban schools established music programs and hired School Band Directors to teach band courses and conduct related activities. Many present-day elementary schools, middle schools, high schools, colleges, and universities provide extensive band and music programs.

Working Conditions

School Band Directors spend the majority of their workday in the school's music rooms. Elementary schools, middle schools, secondary schools, colleges, and universities employ most of these professionals. Some directors teach at several schools. They may travel between the institutions and spend part of a day working with the students in each school. Band directors may also lead school orchestras and teach students to play stringed instruments.

School bands usually perform at various school functions, special programs, and community affairs. Directors accompany the band to these presentations. These professionals may spend much of their time traveling. Students, parents, or other faculty members typically help handle various aspects of a trip, but the band director is responsible for organizing and conducting the excursions.

Hours of Work

School Band Directors may work more hours than some other teachers. Directors hold classes and practice sessions during the regular school hours and may then spend additional time conducting rehearsals after school. On average, these professionals spend about forty-eight hours per week completing teaching duties, preparing for classes and performances, attending meetings, and performing related tasks. They may work additional hours when they conduct special rehearsals, teach private lessons, or travel with the band.

Some band directors work with individual students and the whole band during the school's summer vacation. The school system may sponsor summer band programs, or the director may institute such a program on a private basis. These professionals typically receive additional wages for their summer work.

Ability Required

Band directors need to be accomplished musicians. They should be able to play several different instruments, though some teachers cannot play every instrument in the band. Directors should be able to recognize and hear tone and quality. They should have a good sense of rhythm and be able to present a good stage presence. These teachers need to have a thorough background in music education. They should be able to apply contemporary teaching methods in order to present the subject in a way the students can understand and appreciate. In addition, these professionals need to be able to organize events, pay close attention to details, and gain the cooperation and respect of the students they teach.

Temperament Required

Individuals need to be patient when teaching young people to play an instrument. They should be enthusiastic about music and encourage students to practice and achieve their best during performances. These professionals should enjoy working with students on a one-to-one basis and in a large group. They should also enjoy helping other people develop their musical talents. Directors should be persuasive, tactful, and sincere. In addition, they should enjoy performing in front of audiences.

Education and Training Required

Prospective School Band Directors typically need to be certified as a teacher to work in this position. To be eligible for certification, they should earn a minimum of a bachelor's degree from an accredited school. Most individuals who are interested in this career choose to major in music education during their undergraduate studies. In order to maintain their teaching certificate, professionals need to update their education throughout their career.

Through continuing education, band directors can learn about new developments in teaching and in band music. They can also learn about ways to offer new challenges to their students. Many people in this field choose to take advanced classes or graduate work. Schools may require candidates to have a master's degree for some positions. Colleges, universities, and private music schools hire applicants with a graduate degree to teach music classes.

Finances Required Before Earning

The cost of tuition varies according to the type of school students attend. At public home-state universities, tuition often costs between $6,000 and $16,000 per year. Students from out of state may pay additional fees. At private colleges, tuition can cost from $15,000 to more than $30,000 annually. Individuals should also budget for living expenses, which frequently range from $5,000 to $15,000 annually. Books and supplies may cost about $1,000 each year. Individuals can also benefit from taking private music lessons, which could cost several hundred dollars or more per year.

Financial Aid Information

For a free booklet on financial aid, one may write to or e-mail the following:

Financial Aids for Students
Finney Company
3943 Meadowbrook Road
Minneapolis, Minnesota 55426-4505
feedback@finney-hobar.com

Attractive Features

School Band Directors often feel a sense of satisfaction when they teach individuals to play instruments or when the band successfully performs a concert. Many of these professionals enjoy performing in public. In addition, they may have opportunities to work directly with their students over a period of several years. As a result, they can closely follow their students' progress.

Disadvantages

School Band Directors frequently work more than forty hours a week. Some people dislike the time commitments of this career. These professionals may spend time outside of their regular classes helping students rehearse, working individually with musicians, attending special functions and performances, and participating in meetings. Directors who do a great deal of traveling may spend considerable amounts of time away from home. These professionals may also become involved in extracurricular projects, such as raising funds for band uniforms or trips. Some individuals in this field feel discouraged or disappointed when students do not practice or perform at their highest levels of ability.

Outlook for the Future

The employment market for School Band Directors will likely experience average growth through the year 2010. School funding cuts may affect the expansion of existing band programs, however. These cuts may also contribute to a reduction in the programs schools offer. Candidates for a position in this field will likely find employment opportunities as current teachers and directors retire from the workforce. People can benefit from having marketing and fund-raising knowledge or experience when they promote school bands and try to raise funds for programs.

Licensing, Unions, Organizations

Public schools generally require candidates for teaching positions to be certified. Some parochial and other private schools hire applicants who are not certified. Many School Band Directors become members of a union, such as the American Federation of Teachers or the National Education Association. These individuals can also join professional organizations, including the National Band Association, Inc., the American School Band Directors Association, or other music-related groups.

Suggested Courses in High School

Students who are interested in this career should take as many music classes, especially band courses, as possible in high school. Through these courses, they can prepare for advanced studies of music and develop a knowledge and appreciation for this subject. Students can develop communication and public-speaking skills through English and speech classes. In addition, individuals who plan to pursue a postsecondary degree should take college-preparatory classes, including courses in science, mathematics, social studies, and a foreign language.

Suggested High School Activities

Prospective Band Directors can gain applicable experience for this career by joining the high school band and extracurricular music groups. Some directors offer students opportunities to volunteer as assistants. Through such a position, individuals can learn various techniques involved in playing and performing music. Students can also benefit from participating in other musical activities, such as private instrument lessons. In addition, they may be able to gain applicable experience by volunteering at community centers or summer music camps.

Methods to Enter Work

Most colleges and universities have a placement office to help graduates find available positions in their field. The state department of education and the state teachers' association may be able to provide information about employment opportunities for band directors. Some employers advertise job openings in the classified sections of newspapers, in professional publications, or on the Internet. Unions that represent people in this field may also have information about employment opportunities. In addition, candidates can contact schools for which they would like to work to learn about available positions.

Additional Information

American Federation of Teachers
555 New Jersey Avenue NW
Washington, DC 20001
http://www.aft.org

MENC: The National Association for Music Education
1806 Robert Fulton Drive
Reston, Virginia 20191
http://www.menc.org

National Band Association, Inc.
118 College Drive, Suite 5032
Hattiesburg, Missouri 39406
http://www.nationalbandassociation.org

National Education Association
1201 16th Street NW
Washington, DC 20036-3290
http://www.nea.org

Related Web Sites

Band Director
http://www.banddirector.com
This Web site offers information, articles, and resources related to school bands. Viewers can also access a discussion board, a chat room, and a classified section.

School Band and Orchestra Magazine
http://www.sbomagazine.com
Viewers of this Web site can find articles and resources related to many aspects of directing a school band, including program profiles, teacher surveys, fund-raising activities, grant-writing, educational trends, and music technology.

Testing Your Interests

How can you know if you are suited to this occupation? Ask yourself these questions. If you answer "yes" to most of them and the job sounds interesting, you may want to look into this vocation further as a possible career.

1. Do I appreciate music?

2. Am I skilled in playing at least one instrument?

3. Am I interested in working with and teaching people of various ages and levels of skill?

4. Do I have strong organization skills?

Occupational Guidance

Plumbing Estimator

Description of Work

Plumbing professionals help provide clean, running water and working toilets for people in their homes and businesses. They may be involved in the construction of new homes and businesses and maintain the plumbing in existing structures. Plumbing contracting companies range in size from small firms with a few employees to large firms with hundreds of people specializing in certain types of work. Regardless of their size, many contracting companies rely on the services of Plumbing Estimators.

Plumbing Estimators assess proposed plumbing jobs and estimate their costs. Heating and plumbing contractors usually quote the charges or submit a bid for clients before they begin a job, so they are typically bound by the stated charge. If Plumbing Estimators calculate too high of an estimate, their employing company may lose the job to a competitor. In contrast, a low bid may cause the contractor to lose money on the project.

Plumbing Estimators need to be thoroughly knowledgeable about plumbing and the company for which they work in order to calculate the costs of proposed jobs accurately. They should consider the labor and materials involved in a job and the different types of problems that could arise when completing a project. These professionals typically do not need to be trained plumbers, but they should be familiar with each phase of the work in order to accurately estimate labor time.

Estimators should consider each job carefully, since no two jobs are exactly alike. Each job has a unique layout and working conditions. Large plumbing companies often handle new construction projects. For such projects, they usually install plumbing before other construction employees add the inside walls and floors. Estimators may assess the cost of a project by reviewing blueprints and specifications for the structure that the construction company is building. They closely study the plans and specifications, locate and list the required fixtures such as sinks and toilets, and locate the water and sewage lines and other connections. These individuals measure lengths of pipe according to the scale drawings. They may also specify the diameters of pipes and types of joints. Estimators who work for small plumbing companies may sketch the fixtures, main water and sewage lines, and other connections on a copy of the blueprints, or they may use a computer to sketch these elements. They then review the working drawings and specifications and create a list of the materials their employing company would need to complete the job.

Once they have determined the appropriate amounts and types of materials, Plumbing Estimators need to determine the time and cost of labor for the job. In most shops, these professionals use computers to determine the rough figures for the estimate. They enter the types of materials the company would use for the project and other specifications. A computer program then calculates the cost of the items and how much time the particular job will likely take. Some computer programs also estimate the required lengths of pipe using scale models. Estimators use computer technology to create rough bids. They then consider variables, such as weather conditions and the availability of supplies. They may adjust the rough bid to allow for the likelihood of delays when creating a final estimate.

The costs of materials and labor typically account for the greatest portion of the price for a proposed job, but estimators also need to consider the company's operating and overhead expenses. They generally include a predetermined percentage of each of these costs in their estimate. They may contact different departments within their employing company to obtain accurate numbers. Estimators may also include the margin of company profit in the calculation.

Plumbing Estimators total the component parts of the estimate and then prepare a bid for the job. They usually submit a written offer to the person or group responsible for the building project. These professionals may then attend the public readings of open bids. Some companies manage the bidding process online. Estimators who submit bids for such companies may monitor the process from their computer. Construction companies or building owners may select the company that provides the lowest bid, or they may consider other factors, such as the reliability of a plumbing contract or past experience working with the contractor. Local, state, and federal government agencies may have standardized procedures for accepting or evaluating bids concerning government projects.

If their employing company is awarded the contract for a job, estimators usually give the materials list to the company's project manager. This manager then orders the materials for the job. Plumbing Estimators may work closely with the project manager on proposed plans and explain to the manager how they developed the bid and how they had intended the company to complete the work. They often base an estimate on a particular technique or on the use of specific types of materials. Therefore, the final price of the project may be significantly different from the estimate if crews use different methods or materials. In some companies, Plumbing Estimators serve as project managers in addition to completing their other duties. They may also serve as supervisors or organizers for labor crews, conduct daily assessments of the progress of jobs, answer employees' and clients' questions, and solve problems.

When individuals in this profession estimate jobs for individual home owners, they may speak directly with the prospective client in person or over the telephone. They often visit the home to inspect the existing plumbing and discuss the proposed changes with the client. These professionals may make calculations and provide the home owner with an estimate during the inspection. Jobs for individual home owners can range from installing a garbage disposal unit or new faucets to replacing all the pipes attached to the main sewer and water lines.

Individuals who are interested in this career may also want to read about related occupations, including Plumber (*Occupational Guidance* Vol. VII, Unit 1I, No. 14), Pipefitter (Vol. II, Unit 5H, No. 7), Building Inspector (Vol. IV, Unit 3H, No. 2), and Cost Estimator (Vol. III, Unit 4H, No. 16). Additional construction and engineering technology careers are listed in the *Occupational Guidance* Cluster Index under the classification 05.03 Engineering Technology.

Earnings

Plumbing Estimators' earnings typically vary according to their experience, education, and employer. Entry-level professionals in this field often earn from $28,000 to $36,000 a year. The starting salary for estimators who have a degree in engineering or construction management may range from $36,000 to $48,000 annually. Experienced individuals may earn from $55,000 to more than $75,000 each year.

Most employers in this field offer benefits to full-time employees. Estimators may receive health insurance; paid vacation time, holidays, and sick leave; and retirement plans.

History of Occupation

The ancient Egyptians developed a simple plumbing system. They constructed crude metal pipes and used these pipes to carry water and drainage. The Romans later built an extensive plumbing system. They constructed huge aqueducts to supply cities with water. They also installed public baths and complete drainage systems in cities. Few people had plumbing in their homes, however.

Many cultures did not widely accept the importance or necessity of sanitation until the late 19th century. They often had poorly designed plumbing fixtures that allowed dirty water to enter and contaminate the clean water system. This problem was called *cross connections*. It accounted for nearly all the typhoid fever cases in the United States in the 1930s.

Around the turn of the 20th century, the first laws were enacted requiring plumbers to be licensed. In 1906, The American Society of Sanitary Engineering was established. As the plumbing profession grew, cities established public waterworks. This development allowed people to incorporate indoor plumbing into their homes and businesses.

The plumbing industry continued to expand. Many large companies that handled numerous jobs began to recognize the need for Plumbing Estimators to prepare bids for jobs. These companies initially employed highly skilled plumbers in this position because the individuals had practical knowledge of the labor and materials involved in plumbing procedures. In a short time, however, they started to hire mechanical engineers who had specialized knowledge in the areas of plumbing and heating to work as Plumbing Estimators. Many present-day plumbing contractors continue to hire estimators to help them secure jobs and make a profit.

Working Conditions

Some professionals in this field serve as members of a team with several other individuals. They may spend much of their time in an office and handle estimates for jobs within their specialty area. Other people serve as the only estimator in their company. These professionals may perform a wide variety of duties.

Plumbing Estimators often visit project sites, which can be dirty, dusty, and cluttered. They may supervise plumbers' work daily by checking on the labor crews. They may also spend some time talking with customers.

Individuals in this profession may estimate the costs of projects for people's homes or small businesses on-site. For new construction projects, however, they usually work from plans and specifications in their office. They may spend much of their time on the telephone. Estimators may find their work stressful at times, especially when they need to meet deadlines.

Hours of Work

The standard workweek for most individuals in this profession is from forty to fifty hours. Plumbing companies typically schedule their employees to work Monday through Friday, but some contractors are open on Saturdays as well. Estimators may occasionally need to work overtime to meet deadlines.

Ability Required

Plumbing Estimators need to have organizational, analytical, and planning skills. They need to have an aptitude for mathematics and should be able to read blueprints. These professionals should also have computer skills and be able to use estimating, spreadsheet, and word-processing software. They need to understand the technical and manual aspects of installing plumbing fixtures and equipment. In addition, estimators should have good interpersonal, management, and written and verbal communication skills.

Temperament Required

Plumbing Estimators need to be systematic, precise, detail-oriented, and thorough in their work. They should present a professional and friendly demeanor. Individuals in this career field need to work well with a variety of people. They should have good judgment and self-confidence in making decisions. In addition, estimators need to be comfortable accepting responsibility.

Education and Training Required

About half of Plumbing Estimators gained the skills and experience they needed for this position by first working in other skilled plumbing jobs. Individuals who prepare for this career in this way may need to work for many years before they are promoted to the position of estimator, however.

Other people who want to work as a Plumbing Estimator pursue a postsecondary degree in construction science, construction management, or mechanical or sanitary engineering. Some students work in entry-level positions in the plumbing trade while they earn their degree. Other individuals learn plumbing skills after they have obtained a degree and have begun working in this field.

Finances Required Before Earning

Some individuals who are interested in this career choose to obtain a postsecondary degree. They should budget for the associated educational expenses. At public career and technical schools and community colleges, tuition typically costs from $2,000 to $7,000 annually. Private career and technical schools may charge from $4,000 to $15,000 per year for tuition. Individuals who attend public home-state universities often pay between $6,000 and $16,000 for tuition each year. Students from out of state may pay additional fees. Private colleges may charge from $15,000 to more than $30,000 annually for tuition. Students should also budget for living expenses, which frequently range from $5,000 to $15,000 annually. Books and supplies may cost about $1,000 per year.

Other people advance to the position of Plumbing Estimator after working for several years in a related position. Individuals who want to work as plumbers need to complete an apprenticeship program. Employers typically pay apprentices while they complete the training program.

These individuals need to have enough money to pay for their living expenses until they receive their first paycheck.

Financial Aid Information

For a free booklet on financial aid, one may write to or e-mail the following:

Financial Aids for Students
Finney Company
3943 Meadowbrook Road
Minneapolis, Minnesota 55426-4505
feedback@finney-hobar.com

Attractive Features

Plumbing Estimators may appreciate the challenges and variety of tasks that accompany this career. They may also appreciate the opportunities they have to interact with many different people, including architects, engineers, contractors, construction employees, and home owners. In addition, individuals in this profession typically have a high level of job security.

Disadvantages

People may need to work in related positions for many years before they have opportunities to advance to the position of Plumbing Estimator. Some people are discouraged from entering the field by this level of competition. Estimators may find the detailed nature of this work to be tedious at times. They may also find the level of responsibility that accompanies this career to be stressful.

Outlook for the Future

Employment experts predict that the job market for Plumbing Estimators should be strong through the year 2012. Many metropolitan areas may need to replace their system of water and sanitary lines in the near future. This factor should increase the demand for plumbing professionals. As the construction industry grows, the number of employment opportunities for Plumbing Estimators may also grow. In addition, candidates may find position openings as professionals currently working in the field transfer to other occupations, are promoted, or retire from the workforce. People who have a related postsecondary degree and practical experience will likely have an advantage over other candidates in securing a position in this field.

Licensing, Unions, Organizations

Individuals do not need to be licensed to work as an estimator. They are not required to join unions, either, though some estimators who previously worked as licensed plumbers may maintain their union membership on an associate basis. Many Plumbing Estimators choose to join professional organizations, such as the American Society of Professional Estimators or the Hydronics Institute. The institute is a division of the Gas Appliance Manufacturers Association.

Suggested Courses in High School

Students who are interested in a career as a Plumbing Estimator can benefit from taking mathematics, physics, industrial technology, and computer courses in high school. If their school offers such classes, they may also want to take courses in mechanical or computerized drawing. Through English and speech classes, individuals can improve their communication skills. Students who plan to pursue postsecondary education should also take any remaining college-preparatory classes, including courses in history and a foreign language.

Suggested High School Activities

Prospective Plumbing Estimators can gain applicable experience for this career through activities such as helping to sell raffle tickets or serving as a treasurer for a school club. They can improve their manual dexterity by completing projects through an industrial technology or 4-H club. These individuals can also gain applicable experience by working on home repair projects. They can improve their communication, interpersonal, and teamwork skills by participating in group activities, such as drama, student council, or team athletics.

Methods to Enter Work

Many postsecondary institutions have a placement office. Graduates can contact their school's office for assistance in securing employment in the plumbing industry. Companies may advertise position openings in the classified sections of newspapers or trade journals, on the Internet, or through state or private employment agencies. Individuals may also learn about career opportunities by networking with people involved in the plumbing industry. In addition, candidates can directly contact companies for which they would like to work to inquire about job openings.

Additional Information

Association for the Advancement of Cost Engineering
209 Prairie Avenue, Suite 100
Morgantown, West Virginia 26501
http://www.aacei.org

Plumbing-Heating-Cooling Contractors Educational Foundation
PO Box 6808
Falls Church, Virginia 22040
http://www.phccweb.org

Professional Construction Estimators Association
PO Box 680336
Charlotte, North Carolina 28216
http://www.pcea.org

Society of Cost Estimating and Analysis
101 South Whiting Street, Suite 201
Alexandria, Virginia 22304
http://www.sceaonline.net

Related Web Sites

Plumbing & Mechanical **Magazine**
http://www.pmmag.com
This Web site provides industry news and columns and information about publications, new products, and additional resources.

ThePlumber.com
http://www.theplumber.com/index.html
Viewers of this Web site can find a selection of articles, discussion forums, and information about industry safety issues and the history of plumbing.

Testing Your Interests

How can you know if you are suited to this occupation? Ask yourself these questions. If you answer "yes" to most of them and the job sounds interesting, you may want to look into this vocation further as a possible career.

1. Do I have an aptitude for mathematics?

2. Am I detail-oriented, precise, and thorough in my work?

3. Do I have mechanical skills?

4. Do I enjoy performing planning and analysis activities?

5. Do I have good communication and interpersonal skills, and can I work well with a variety of people?

Published by Finney Company, Minneapolis, Minnesota 55426-4505
© Finney Company 2005

Occupational Guidance

Product Demonstrator

Description of Work

Some product manufacturers contract with marketing service companies to provide consumers with demonstrations of their products. These companies may market a broad range of items, from sports cars to kitchen knives to food items to industrial-strength cleaning products. Marketing service companies employ Product Demonstrators to introduce consumers to manufacturers' products. These employees may work in many different types of environments. As an example, a Product Demonstrator may set up a stand in a grocery store and invite shoppers to taste foods such as ice cream, cheese and cracker combinations, or a new pickle relish. The manufacturers of the food products typically provide free samples for the demonstrations in an effort to encourage consumers to buy the products.

Manufacturers that want to increase their sales of specialty items like fishing lures or luxury products like perfume may hire demonstrators who can present an image to complement the merchandise. For example, the demonstrator for the fishing lure may have a beard and wear a plaid shirt. The demonstrator for the perfume may be dressed in formalwear and offer to spray samples on customers of an upscale department store.

Product demonstrations are typically expensive promotions for manufacturers. Therefore, companies may choose to limit such promotions to a short period of time, often about two days. When a manufacturer gives a marketing service company a contract to demonstrate or give away an item, the marketing company contacts the necessary number of demonstrators and arranges the employees' work schedules. The company may send demonstrators to numerous establishments throughout a multistate area for a single day, or they may assign several people to work at a county fair or in a trade show booth for a full week. Demonstrators usually work as independent contractors. A marketing company may assign them a specified number of hours in which to demonstrate a single product.

Marketing service companies typically give advance notice to demonstrators regarding the product they are going to market and the site at which they need to work. If an individual is assigned to demonstrate a food product in a grocery store, this employee may need to bring cooking equipment, utensils, a cutting board, display platters, and an apron to the job site. The demonstrator usually wears attractive, comfortable clothing and footwear. The individual may receive a quick orientation to the product over the telephone. During this orientation, the demonstrator may learn information such as the temperature to use for heating a pizza or the appropriate size of cup to use for juice samples. If manufacturers are promoting the nutritional value of a product, demonstrators may have sheets of recipes or information about the calorie, sodium, or fat content for the item to give to consumers.

Individuals who demonstrate products with which they are unfamiliar may learn how to use the items through orientations that manufacturing sales representatives conduct. Such orientations can last up to three hours. Individual stores may also hire Product Demonstrators. For example, a department store may hire an experienced chef or nutritionist to demonstrate a new type of stove or microwave or give a series of cooking lessons to consumers who purchase the appliances.

For some promotions, Product Demonstrators may need to wear a costume. For example, these individuals may dress as a cupcake, a hot dog, an elf, or Santa Claus to draw consumer's attention. For some promotions, they may simply hand out coupons to passing consumers. For other promotions, these individuals may give away samples of a product in public places, such as beaches or parks.

The most common types of promotions with which Product Demonstrators work involve food products at grocery stores. Demonstrators need to be friendly to shoppers and try to make contact with as many people as possible who pass the display. These individuals may talk with consumers about the item and answer their questions. Demonstrators typically need to stay near the display and remain alert for opportunities to promote the product, regardless of whether the store is busy.

Before they begin some promotions, demonstrators may need to call the store to ensure that the product is in stock.

GOE 08.02.05/O*Net 49032A
O*Net-Soc 41-9011.00

They may also confirm that the manufacturer's arrangements for the display have arrived at the site. These individuals typically plan to arrive at the assigned location early, especially on the first day, to set up the display area. They may occasionally need to adjust or alter their plans to suit the environment and supplies.

The specific duties individuals in this profession perform may vary greatly according to the type of product they are demonstrating. For example, a person who is giving away samples of bacon may use an electric frying pan and tongs and need to arrange a platter. This individual also typically needs to wear plastic gloves before they can handle the food. The demonstrator may count the packages of bacon on display and assess how many packages are in the storage area of the store before and after the demonstration period. Through this process, this individual can determine how many packages customers have purchased that day. Grocery stores usually provide the food and paper products demonstrators use. These individuals may choose to have additional supplies of these items in case they give away an unexpectedly high amount of samples or there is a miscommunication with the store. Before demonstrators leave a store, they usually need to complete a data sheet listing the number of packages the store sold and the number they used in the demonstration. They may also add information regarding comments customers made about the product.

Supervisors of Product Demonstrators may travel to different locations throughout their workday to observe the work of their employees. They often check on new demonstrators and visit with as many experienced staff members as possible. These professionals need to make sure the demonstrators are following company procedures, demonstrating the products according to the specifications of the manufacturers, and cooperating with the stores' management personnel. They are generally responsible for making sure employees are promoting a positive image of the marketing company.

In addition to demonstrating products, individuals in this profession may perform other jobs in stores, such as stocking shelves with a manufacturer's product or working as mystery shoppers. When they serve as mystery shoppers, these individuals travel to different stores to monitor the way the stores are displaying a manufacturer's products. They may also compare the prices of competing products. Mystery shoppers may visit up to one hundred stores in two weeks to record the necessary information.

Individuals who are interested in this career may also want to read about related occupations, including Retail Salesperson (*Occupational Guidance* Vol. III, Unit 2I, No. 16), Manufacturer's Representative (Vol. VII, Unit 1I, No. 8), and Specialty Salesperson (Vol. VII, Unit 1I, No. 11).

Earnings

Product Demonstrators typically earn an hourly wage, which can vary according to the type of promotion on which they work. Individuals who distribute samples in a grocery store, for example, frequently earn from $7 to $9 an hour. Demonstrators who work at a trade show booth often earn from $10 to $14 per hour. Highly experienced demonstrators who work with complicated cooking equipment or high-tech electronics may earn up to $20 an hour. In addition to their wages, individuals in this profession may earn commission on product sales.

Most Product Demonstrators work part-time on a contract basis. Therefore, they do not typically receive benefits. Some individuals in this profession are full-time employees, however. If their employers provide benefits, these demonstrators may receive health insurance and paid holidays, vacation time, and sick leave.

History of Occupation

Country peddlers were some of the earlist American Product Demonstrators. These individuals traveled throughout rural areas in the 1800s and sold items such as bolts of calico, pots and pans, and fiddle strings. Consumers could also buy goods from small shopkeepers or street vendors.

In the late 1800s, the Industrial Revolution and the mechanization of agriculture allowed manufacturers to introduce many new products to American consumers. Manufacturers of farm equipment and machinery, for example, employed Product Demonstrators to persuade farmers to switch from traditional methods involving hand tools to steam- and gasoline-powered plows and harvesters.

Some dry goods stores, such as the establishment that R. H. Macy owned in New York City, expanded and became the first department stores. By the 1940s, manufacturers and wholesalers began employing agents to travel around the United States and market the company's goods to retail stores. These salespeople often traveled on railroads, which manufacturers also used to transport products more quickly and reliably than they had in the past.

Companies began to focus on improving their sales techniques to compete in the growing retail markets. The National Cash Register Company, for example, asked its best salesperson to explain to other company employees how he had secured so many sales. He taught other company representatives a rehearsed sales pitch.

People have continued to study and learn about effective sales and marketing techniques. Many manufacturers develop promotions involving Product Demonstrators to introduce new items to consumers. Individuals in this profession may promote a range of items, including home computers, food products, appliances, lawnmowers, specialty automobiles, and many other items.

Working Conditions

Product Demonstrators interact with many different people when they promote products. They may work in busy and noisy environments with large numbers of consumers. These individuals may be stationed at a grocery store, a trade show, a county or state fair booth, the showroom of an automobile dealership, an open exhibit hall, or another location. Depending on the products they are promoting, they may occasionally work outdoors in a recreation area. These individuals often do not work under direct supervision. They may need to stand for many hours at a time.

Hours of Work

Most demonstrators work part-time. They may be on call and receive limited notice about assignments. These individuals' work hours can vary considerably, depending on the items they promote. Demonstrators who distribute samples in grocery stores usually work during the day on weekends. They may also work during the day or in the evening on weekdays. Individuals who work at trade shows often work on weekends. They may be assigned to a fair exhibit or convention booth for a period of time ranging from a few days to several weeks.

Ability Required

Product Demonstrators should have good listening and communication skills. They need to be knowledgeable about the products they are promoting. They should have a good memory for facts and be able to effectively present a product's selling points. For some demonstrations, individuals may need to have basic cooking skills. Demonstrators should have physical stamina to stand for many hours at a time. They should also be in good health, particularly if they work with food items. In addition, some employers require these individuals to have a valid driver's license to travel to different work sites and transport equipment.

Temperament Required

Product Demonstrators should enjoy talking with many different people. They should present a poised and professional demeanor when promoting products. These individuals should be persuasive and not become offended if consumers do not want to sample or purchase their products. They should be tactful when interacting with people who return repeatedly for samples. In addition, Product Demonstrators should work well independently. They need to remain calm in busy environments and be patient if there are few consumers to sample the product.

Education and Training Required

Many companies require applicants for a position in this field to have a high school diploma or the equivalent, though some marketing firms hire people who are in high school to promote products. Marketing service companies may provide orientation programs and some on-the-job training for new employees. Individuals who have an associate degree may have an advantage in securing assignments, particularly if their education relates to the types of products they are demonstrating. People who attend modeling school can learn about presentation methods and techniques to enhance their personal appearance.

Finances Required Before Earning

Employers do not typically require candidates for a position as a Product Demonstrators to have postsecondary education. Therefore, individuals who enter this field need to have enough money to pay for their living expenses until they receive their first paycheck.

People who do choose to earn a postsecondary degree should budget for educational expenses. At public career and technical schools and community colleges, tuition may cost from $2,000 to $7,000 per year. Private career and technical schools often charge from $4,000 to $15,000 annually for tuition. Students should also budget for living expenses, which frequently range from $5,000 to $15,000 annually. Books and supplies may cost an additional $1,000 per year.

Financial Aid Information

For a free booklet on financial aid, one may write to or e-mail the following:

Financial Aids for Students
Finney Company
3943 Meadowbrook Road
Minneapolis, Minnesota 55426-4505
feedback@finney-hobar.com

Attractive Features

Some people appreciate the part-time and temporary nature of this career. They have the option of turning down assignments if they dislike the assignment or are busy with other projects. Product Demonstrators may also appreciate the opportunities to interact with many different people and work in a variety of job sites.

Disadvantages

If there are few people in a store or other job site, Product Demonstrators may find their work boring. In contrast, they may feel stressed if there are many people waiting for samples. Individuals who are uncomfortable standing for several hours at a time or who do not like moving to different job sites may not be suited for this career. In addition, people in this profession may dislike the lack of financial stability; they do not usually know how many hours they are going to work each week.

Outlook for the Future

Employment experts predict that the job market for Product Demonstrators will likely remain strong through the year 2012. Individuals may find position openings as people currently working in the field are promoted, transfer to other occupations, or retire from the workforce. The national economy impacts the number of employment opportunities for demonstrators, however. Therefore, the rate of job growth in this field may slow during economic downturns.

Licensing, Unions, Organizations

Product Demonstrators do not need to be licensed to work in this field, and they do not usually become members of unions. Employees of a product manufacturer may have opportunities to join an in-house group that promotes the manufacturer's product, however.

Suggested Courses in High School

Students can gain applicable skills for this career through courses in speech, acting, marketing, and family and consumer sciences. Individuals who want to specialize in working with computers can benefit from taking computer and keyboarding courses in high school. They may have opportunities to work with machinery and other types of electronic equipment through industrial technology classes, particularly courses in mechanics and electronics.

Suggested High School Activities

Product Demonstrators frequently interact with the public. Students can improve their communication and interpersonal skills by participating in team sports, student council, drama, and debate activities. They can gain experience working with products and consumers through a part-time or summer job at a retail establishment.

Methods to Enter Work

Marketing service companies may advertise available positions for Product Demonstrators through the classified sections of newspapers or on the Internet. Candidates can also directly contact companies for which they would like to work to inquire about employment opportunities. They may find the contact information for such organizations in telephone business directories, on the Internet, or by talking

with Product Demonstrators they encounter in stores or at other locations.

Additional Information

National Association for Retail Marketing Services
PO Box 906
Plover, Wisconsin 54467-0906
http://www.narms.com

Related Web Sites

Promotion Marketing Association, Inc.
http://www.pmalink.org
This Web site features information about task forces and chapters of the organization, certification opportunities, related publications, and employment opportunities in the marketing field.

Trade Show Exhibitors Association
http://www.tsea.org
Viewers of this Web site can find information about educational opportunities, trade show and marketing careers, and additional resources.

Testing Your Interests

How can you know if you are suited to this occupation? Ask yourself these questions. If you answer "yes" to most of them and the job sounds interesting, you may want to look into this vocation further as a possible career.

1. Do I enjoy interacting with many different people?

2. Am I interested in working in retail environments?

3. Do I have strong communication and listening skills?

4. Am I in good physical health, and do I have the stamina necessary to stand for several hours at a time?

5. Can I work well without direct supervision?

Published by Finney Company, Minneapolis, Minnesota 55426-4505
© Finney Company 2005

Occupational Guidance

Washington Correspondent

Description of Work

Washington Correspondents cover the news that happens in the capital city of the United States. These professionals may work for a press association; a television or radio network; a large metropolitan daily newspaper that maintains its own Washington, DC, bureau; or a bureau that serves several newspapers, radio or television stations, or magazines.

Correspondents who work for a wire service, a major newspaper or broadcast group, or a broadcast network usually have a regular beat, or news source, to cover. For example, an individual in this profession may specialize in reporting on the White House, the State Department, the Pentagon, other federal departments, or Congress. Correspondents who work for small newspapers or individual broadcast outlets typically cover news of regional interest.

The White House is one of the most demanding beats in Washington, DC. Reporters who cover the White House need to attend daily briefings to collect information about the President's schedule, policies, and staff and to ask the press secretary about national and world events. Once they have gathered the information and written a story, newspaper correspondents relay the news story to their editors via computer. They typically keep in continuous contact with their editors through e-mail and cell phone technology. Television reporters work with producers, news directors, and photojournalists when they collect information and report a story. Editors and news directors also send queries for reporters to answer. Professionals in this field constantly work under the pressure of a deadline. White House reporters may frequently travel to domestic and international locations with the President. These correspondents also cover presidential campaigns, which happen every four years. During the campaigns, they may need to travel continuously. Individuals who specialize in reporting on the White House typically try to become acquainted with White House staff members in order to stay continuously informed about the President's activities.

Many correspondents who work for major newspapers or networks, wire services, and foreign publications cover the Department of State and attend press conferences at this location. Reporters in this profession may also cover other government agencies. Officials in various agencies frequently hold press conferences and issue mass amounts of printed news releases. Correspondents may need to sift through a great deal of information in order to avoid missing important stories. They may need to do background research in order to explain and put official announcements, policy changes, and proposals into context.

Washington Correspondents can also cover events at the capitol building. When Congress is in session, reporters can speak directly with members of the House of Representatives in the Speaker's Lobby just outside the chamber. They can interview senators in the lobby off the Senate floor. Lawmakers often assign their aides the task of handling press inquiries.

In addition to interviewing members of Congress or their aides, reporters may cover the committee meetings of both houses of Congress. Committee groups usually meet in the morning. Correspondents listen to the testimony during the meetings. Afterward, they may interview witnesses and legislators involved in the meetings. Later in the day, reporters typically go to the House or Senate, which generally meet at noon. From the press galleries, they can listen to debates and speeches. There are pressrooms located nearby that are equipped with telephones and computers for correspondents' use.

Regardless of their specific beat, correspondents generally spend a great deal of time reading newspapers, government reports, news releases from officials and special interest groups, wire service reports, and the Congressional Record. They also spend time talking with experts, bureaucrats, and politicians. Many of these professionals try to stay informed about developments that would interest a specific geographic area or individuals in a particular field. In addition to their other duties, correspondents may answer queries from their employer's home office and develop feature stories. Some individuals in this profession also write columns that appear regularly in their newspapers or work as news analysts for radio and television stations.

Individuals who are interested in this career need to obtain several years of experience in the journalism field before they would be eligible for a position as a Washington

Correspondent. Some people start working in this field as a Newspaper Reporter (*Occupational Guidance* Vol. III, Unit 4H, No. 4), Editorial Assistant (Vol. VII, Unit 5H, No. 10), or Radio/Television Newscaster (Vol. I, Unit 5H, No. 10) for a weekly newspaper or small television or radio station.

Individuals who are interested in a supervisory position in the journalism field may also want to read about the occupations of City Editor (*Occupational Guidance* Vol. II, Unit 4H, No. 13) and Radio/Television News Director (Vol. VII, Unit 2I, No. 17). There are additional related careers listed under 11.08 Communications in the *Occupational Guidance* Cluster Index.

Earnings

Washington Correspondents often have somewhat higher earnings than journalists who cover other beats. Their earnings can vary greatly according to the employer for which they work, however. Reporters who work for a radio station may earn less than professionals in the television industry, for example. Small-market media companies typically do not pay as much as large-market employers. In general, reporters earn between $22,000 and $47,000 each year. Washington Correspondents may earn from $33,000 to more than $70,000 annually. High-profile correspondents may earn substantially more than $70,000 a year.

Many full-time correspondents receive benefits in addition to their salaries. Employers frequently provide health insurance; paid holidays, vacation time, and sick leave; and a retirement plan. Individuals who need to live in the Washington, DC, area while they are covering stories may receive an allowance from their employer to help pay for housing costs.

History of Occupation

The first American newspaper was published in the colonies in the 17th century. Government authorities suppressed the publication four days after it appeared. The first continuously published periodical was started in the early 1700s. In 1776, there were about two-dozen newspapers that covered the continuing political and economic expansion of the colonies. By the end of the Revolutionary War in 1783, forty-three newspapers were in printed circulation. There are currently about 1,500 daily newspapers and about 7,500 weekly papers in the United States.

Washington was a small southern settlement with a population of a few thousand people when the U.S. government decided to make it the capital city. Around 1800, the federal government established the capitol building on a site near the Potomac River. Newspaper editors in other parts of the country initially waited for the Washington, DC, newspapers to arrive by stagecoach and then rewrote the news to publish in their own papers. A press corps gradually began to develop. The inventions of the railroad and telegraph helped correspondents send news from Washington, DC, to other parts of the country.

Present-day news organizations can transmit news reports instantly around the world via satellite. Satellite technology was first used in 1982 to cover the Falkland Islands/Great Britain conflict. Since that time, Satellite News Gathering (SNG) has upgraded to digital technology and uses Internet protocol. Broadcast and print correspondents throughout the world use this technology. Washington Correspondents can travel with the President or report on various events in Washington, DC, and send news articles back to their employer's home office to meet daily deadlines.

Working Conditions

Many Washington Correspondents have office space in the National Press Building, which is located a few blocks from the White House. Other professionals in this field have offices elsewhere in central Washington, DC. Beat reporters typically spend much of their time away from their bureaus. They may use the telephones, fax machines, televisions, and computers in the office facilities and pressrooms at the Capitol and White House, though these spaces are often crowded and cramped. Wire services and some big newspapers have their own direct-to-the-office telephones in these pressrooms. Some beat reporters who work for such employers have an assigned desk in one of the pressrooms. General assignment and special correspondents might need to travel throughout the city to report on stories and meet with officials in various government departments. Television and radio correspondents may report live from different scenes or prepare tapes to send to the main office via satellite or microwave link. Professionals in this field constantly work under the pressure of deadlines.

Some Washington Correspondents travel with political candidates and attend national political conventions. White House correspondents usually go to different locations with the President. Air Force One can carry a limited number of individuals, so correspondents may take turns traveling on the jet. About one dozen print and broadcast reporters and photojournalists can fly with the President. The other reporters need to fly by chartered plane. They typically join a motorcade at their destination.

Hours of Work

Washington Correspondents may frequently have long workdays, depending on the nature of their daily assignments. White House reporters often start their workday when the press secretary holds the daily press conference or when the first of the President's visitors arrives. When the President travels, these professionals may need to arrive at Andrews Air Force Base before dawn for security screening. Each administration in the White House may follow a different schedule, but correspondents are generally responsible for reporting on the events at the White House throughout the day.

Washington Correspondents may be on call outside of their regular work hours. Their home office may contact them at any point in the day or night to cover a big news event. Correspondents who specialize in covering Congress typically start their workday when congressional committees meet, which is usually not earlier than 8:30 a.m. These professionals then remain at the Capitol until Congress adjourns in the afternoon or evening. Individuals who cover federal offices adjust their schedules so they can cover press conferences and other relevant events.

After they have gathered information for their story, they may return to their office to write and file the article or they may send the story to the home office via computer. Washington Correspondents may frequently have to work weekends and holidays, depending on the type of events that occur.

Ability Required

Washington Correspondents need to be able to work quickly, accurately, and impartially under pressure. They need to have excellent writing skills and should be able to explain issues and events clearly and concisely. These professionals should have interpersonal skills and be able to work well with a variety of people. They often rely on other people to provide them with news sources. Reporters need to be able to cover a wide range of stories. They should have good physical stamina and be able to handle stress well.

Temperament Required

Journalists should be inquisitive, thorough, and analytical when researching and reporting about events. They need to remain alert for possible news stories and be flexible in responding to the stories. These individuals need to be intelligent and responsible. They should be persistent in pursuing a story and in questioning people who are reluctant to give them information. Correspondents need to have good judgment in determining the validity of a news source and in deciding how much they should emphasize particular information in an article. These professionals should remain calm and composed under extreme pressure. They should be self-motivated and resourceful.

Education and Training Required

Individuals need to have a minimum of a bachelor's degree to work in this field. Many correspondents earn a graduate degree. Some editors and news directors prefer to hire candidates with a degree in journalism or mass communications, while other employers prefer to hire applicants who have a liberal arts degree with a background in English and writing. Washington Correspondents need to be able to explain the processes of government clearly and accurately, so they should have knowledge of specialized fields such as political science and economics. Individuals who want to work as Washington Correspondents typically need to have a minimum of five years experience in the field of journalism before they can advance to this position.

Finances Required Before Earning

Individuals who are interested in this field should plan to pursue a minimum of a bachelor's degree. At public home-state universities, undergraduate tuition often costs from $6,000 to $16,000 a year. Students from out of state may pay additional fees. Private colleges may charge from $15,000 to more than $30,000 a year for undergraduate tuition. Students should also budget for living expenses, which frequently range from $5,000 to $15,000 per year. Books and supplies may cost about $1,000 per year.

Some prospective correspondents earn a master's degree in journalism. Graduate school tuition usually costs about the same as or slightly more than undergraduate tuition. Graduate students may have opportunities to work as a teaching or research assistant to help offset the costs of their education.

Financial Aid Information

Individuals can access information about scholarships for students pursuing a career in journalism from the following organization:

The Dow Jones Newspaper Fund, Inc.
PO Box 300
Princeton, New Jersey 08543-0300
http://djnewspaperfund.dowjones.com

For a free booklet on financial aid, one may write to or e-mail the following:

Financial Aids for Students
Finney Company
3943 Meadowbrook Road
Minneapolis, Minnesota 55426-4505
feedback@finney-hobar.com

Attractive Features

Many people in this profession find their work exciting and rewarding. They may have opportunities to interact with a wide variety of people, from the U.S. President and other world leaders to citizens of Washington DC. These professionals have a great deal of variety in their work and rarely perform routine tasks. Many correspondents gain a sense of satisfaction in feeling that they are helping to preserve democracy by reporting on government affairs.

Disadvantages

Some correspondents who are stationed in Washington, DC, for many years lose touch with people in other areas of the United States. As a result, their writing may become stale or prone to pretension. Reporters typically receive a great deal of criticism about their work, and not all of the criticism is constructive. Individuals in this profession continuously work under the pressure of deadlines and may find their job highly stressful. After each election, Washington Correspondents may have to establish new sources and build relationships with newly elected officials and their staff members.

Washington, DC, has a higher cost of living than many other cities in the United States. Reporters may have difficulty finding conveniently located and affordable housing. Some people dislike the climate of the capital city, particularly during the hot and humid summers.

Outlook for the Future

The employment market for Washington Correspondents will likely continue to be extremely competitive. Individuals will probably continue to need to have several years of work experience before they can advance to this position. People who specialize in covering political issues and events while they are gaining experience may have an advantage over other reporters in securing a position as a Washington Correspondent. Journalists with limited experience may be able to secure a position in this city by working for newsletters or specialty publications produced in Washington, DC, and then applying for positions with major news media.

Licensing, Unions, Organizations

Individuals do not need to join a union to work in this field, but many Washington Correspondents choose to become members of the Newspaper Guild. Reporters who routinely cover the President need to pass a background investigation that the Secret Service administers. They then receive a pass that allows them access to the White House. Individuals who specialize in covering Congress receive a special pass that allows them access to the congressional media galleries. With this pass, they are also allowed to enter some areas of the Capitol that are off limits to the public. In addition, journalists who cover the Defense Department need to get a special pass to enter the Pentagon.

Correspondents who report on the White House can join the White House Correspondents Association. Some journalists in this field become members of a state organization in Washington, DC, in order to have opportunities to interact with lawmakers, lobbyists, and other officials from their home-office area.

Suggested Courses in High School

Students who want to enter the field of journalism should take college-preparatory courses, including classes in science, mathematics, English, social studies, and a foreign language. They may also want to enroll in additional English and writing classes. Through history and civics courses, individuals can learn about government processes. They can develop computer skills and learn to use different software programs though computer courses.

Suggested High School Activities

Prospective journalists can benefit from gaining experience in writing for a publication, such as a school yearbook or newspaper. They can learn about government procedures by becoming involved in the student government at their school. They can also learn about politics by volunteering to help with political campaigns.

Methods to Enter Work

Individuals typically need to have several years of experience before they can advance to a position as a Washington Correspondent. Colleges and universities may offer placement services to help graduates find an entry-level position or an internship. Through an internship, individuals may be able to make employment contacts in the field. Candidates for a job as an editorial assistant, production assistant, or reporter can apply directly to newspapers and television or radio stations for which they would like to work. Some employers advertise available positions in the classified sections of newspapers, on the Internet, or through state and private employment agencies. After gaining several years of experience and submitting consistently high-quality work, journalists may be able to secure a position as a Washington Correspondent.

Additional Information

National Newspaper Association
PO Box 7540
Columbia, Missouri 65205-7540
http://www.nna.org

Society of Professional Journalists
3909 North Meridian Street
Indianapolis, Indiana 46208
http://www.spj.org

Related Web Sites

Newspaper Guild–CWA
http://www.newsguild.org
This Web site features information about newspaper careers and membership in this organization.

White House Correspondents Association
http://www.whca.net
Viewers of this Web site can find information about scholarship opportunities and industry awards.

Testing Your Interests

How can you know if you are suited to this occupation? Ask yourself these questions. If you answer "yes" to most of them and the job sounds interesting, you may want to look into this vocation further as a possible career.

1. Am I inquisitive and curious about people and events?

2. Am I interested in politics and government affairs?

3. Can I be objective in reporting facts?

4. Can I explains ideas and events clearly and precisely through writing?

5. Do I have strong research skills?

Published by Finney Company, Minneapolis, Minnesota 55426-4505
© Finney Company 2005

Occupational Guidance

Commercial Diver

Description of Work

Commercial Divers work below the surfaces of rivers, lakes, and oceans. They are often involved in construction, inspection, search and rescue, or salvage projects. These professionals generally specialize in diving in either inland or offshore environments. They have the option of using three modes of diving: scuba, surface-supplied air or mixed gas, and bell diving.

People who specialize in inland diving perform their work in waterways, rivers, lakes, and other inland bodies of water. Although such bodies of water are often shallow, divers may face various hazards in their work. They often dive into extremely cold water and have limited or no visibility. In addition, these professionals may come into contact with debris of unknown origin.

Individuals who specialize in offshore diving perform most of their work in oceans or seas. Most of these professionals are involved in maintaining and supporting the oil and gas industries. For example, they may work for a petroleum operation in the Gulf of Mexico. Divers typically have better visibility in the ocean than in inland waters. Offshore professionals face increased risks of decompression sickness because of the depths in which they work, however.

For commercial scuba diving, professionals use a self-contained underwater breathing apparatus (SCUBA). They may choose this type of gear for jobs in optimum conditions that require a short amount of time to complete and that are at shallow depths in which they are not concerned with the effects of decompression.

For some jobs, professionals use a surface-supplied air or mixed-gas diving apparatus. They receive breathing air or gas, communications, lighting power, video camera power, and other support from the surface through such equipment. An umbilical cable on the device provides a breathing hose, communications line, and a *pneumofathometer* hose, which regulates air and registers a diver's depth. If an individual loses voice communications, the diver can communicate with surface support through line-pull signals.

In bell diving, Commercial Divers may use two types of diving bells. A Class II bell is a simple open-bottom diving bell. In this structure, divers can be lowered to an underwater work site. Once they complete their work, they travel back to the surface of a support barge, ship, or platform in this bell. A Class II bell has an umbilical cable to the surface, provides a supply of breathing gases in large cylinders, and may include tool baskets and lights. Divers use this structure for in-water decompression stops as the bell rises to the surface.

A Class I bell is a complicated submersible compression chamber. Diving professionals work within the bell, which is a self-contained pressure vessel. Through this vessel, they have access to onboard breathing gas, heaters, lights, communications equipment, sensors, and controls. A Class I bell is attached to a large deck decompression chamber on board the support ship or barge.

Saturation diving is a form of bell diving. In this type of diving, professionals have access to a submersible decompression chamber and a deck decompression chamber. They remain in a vessel at the pressure of the underwater work environment for the duration of a project, which might last from several days to several weeks. The divers saturate with breathing gases at certain points of dives. These individuals then require one lengthy decompression period at the end of each dive. With this method of diving, people can work at water depths ranging from 160 feet to 1,000 feet.

Divers need to wear special helmets. These helmets are attached directly to metal neck collars, called neck dams. Individuals receive steady supplies of air and can communicate with crews on the surface through neck dams. An air compressor above the surface forces air through an air hose into the helmet. The air also makes a diver's suit somewhat buoyant and helps equalize the pressure water exerts as the individual goes down and works below the surface. Commercial Divers wear vulcanized rubber suits or neoprene suits that are fitted with rubber cuffs and collars. They also wear weighted belts.

GOE 05.10.01/O*Net 85999F

O*Net-So 49-9092.00

Tenders are entry-level employees in this field. These individuals remain on the decks of ships and handle the topside aspects of dive operations and support procedures. They carefully watch the compressors and maintain communication with divers in the water. Divers may relay information to tenders as they descend or work below the surface. If these professionals have any problems or want to come to the surface, they signal the tenders for the ascent.

The types of tasks divers perform underwater vary according to the kind of project on which they are working. For example, an individual may inspect the pilings of a bridge that has weakened or that shows signs of structural failure. This professional descends to the level of the pilings and checks their condition for signs of erosion, decay, damage, or partial collapse. For such jobs, divers typically make a visual inspection. In some cases, however, they may need to collect samples of the piling materials or the ground around the pilings so people on the surface can study them.

Commercial Divers may also work on underwater construction projects that involve structures like pipelines, docks, or piers. Some divers perform welding or metal-cutting work under water. Individuals in this profession may also help maintain structures by inspecting them periodically or when problems occur. Through such inspections, they may be able to prevent extensive damage to the structures.

Many divers are involved in salvage work. They may raise sunken vessels from the water or salvage cargoes of ships that cannot be brought to the water surface. Salvage divers also help raise objects such as automobiles, outboard motors, and other items to the surfaces of inland waters. For a heavy object, these professionals may attach a chain or rope to the item so a winch can pull it up. They may need to cut away debris that is holding the object or fasten special crossbars on the item to hold a chain in place.

Some Commercial Divers inspect *caissons*, which are the watertight chambers that companies use for underwater construction. These professionals may check the inside of these structures in order to detect leaks that could cause serious damage. They routinely inspect the caissons for new bridges. When digging crews work on storm sewers and other aboveground installations, they may accidentally cut through the water table of the area. As a result, water may rise in the caissons. Companies may then rely on divers to inspect the structures.

Some Commercial Divers inspect construction by operating video cameras underwater. Other professionals in this field are involved in underwater demolition projects. Divers may operate small shops in addition to performing underwater work. At such shops, individuals may sell and repair scuba equipment, fill tanks, and give diving instructions to beginners.

People who are interested in this career may also want to read about related occupations, including Underwater Photographer (*Occupational Guidance* Vol. VIII, Unit 3H, No. 11), Underwater Archaeologist (Vol. VIII, Unit 5H, No. 4), and Lifeguard-Water Safety Instructor (Vol. VI, Unit 2I, No. 16).

Earnings

Commercial Divers' incomes typically vary according to the types of projects on which they work, the depth of dives they complete, the location of the work, their area of specialization, and their level of experience. Some divers are paid by a rate per foot descended. Professionals who have several years of experience may earn from $28,000 to more than $48,000 annually. Saturation divers generally earn the highest level of wages in this field. Some divers work as independent contractors and charge a fee or daily rate.

Individuals who work full-time for companies often receive benefits such as health insurance and paid vacation time. Self-employed divers need to pay for their own benefits from their earnings.

History of Occupation

People have used diving techniques for thousands of years. Around 330 B.C., Alexander the Great commanded divers to destroy the defenses of the island city of Tyre in ancient Phoenicia. Pliny the Elder was an ancient Roman writer from the first century A.D. He described an underwater breathing device, which was a type of snorkel, in one of his first books.

In the following centuries, people experimented with many types of breathing devices in their attempts to explore underwater depths. The force pump, which compressed air, was refined in the 1780s. This device became the first practical machine for use in diving. It forced air through an air hose and enabled divers to travel deeper and remain underwater longer than was previously possible. Around 1819, the German inventor Augustus Siebe invented the diving helmet, and modern deep-sea diving began.

The diving helmet allowed people to have additional freedom underwater, but it was cumbersome and awkward. Divers continued to look for improved methods and equipment. In the 1940s, Jacques-Yves Cousteau and Emile Gagnon of France developed a self-contained breathing device for divers, which they called the *Aqua-Lung*. Many people continue to use this patented device.

Such developments contributed to increasing numbers of employment opportunities for Commercial Divers. People began to more fully understand the possibilities of underwater installations than they had in the past. Companies started to rely on divers to assist in construction and inspection projects. Commercial Divers continue to work on such projects in addition to salvage and search and rescue efforts.

Working Conditions

The work environments for professionals in this field may vary according to the type of ship from which they work, the equipment they use, and whether they own a shop. If their equipment malfunctions, divers could be in serious danger, so they typically check their apparatuses meticulously before each dive. These individuals may also face dangers from sea animals or sharp objects that can puncture their suit, damage their equipment, or cut an air hose or lifeline. Divers should make sure they have access to multiple sources of air to breathe. They may need to work in black water, or water that has no visibility, at times. These professionals may also work in confined spaces.

Hours of Work

The hours Commercial Divers work vary according to the types of jobs they complete and the depths to which they dive. They may work underwater for one or two hours and then spend several hours rising slowly from a deep dive. For other jobs, they may spend five to six hours completing complicated tasks. These professionals also spend some time on the surface checking their equipment and preparing tanks and other gear for future dives.

Many offshore divers work twelve-hour shifts. They may have a rotating schedule. Divers who need to decompress usually require twenty-four hours between shifts to let the remaining gas escape.

Ability Required

Commercial Divers need to have good eyesight and hearing. They should be able to remain calm and take a logical approach to problems while underwater. These professionals need to have excellent health and good body coordination and physical stamina. They should be proficient swimmers, especially if they use self-contained apparatuses. Divers also need to have mechanical skills. They should understand and be able to apply physics, mathematics, physiology, and treatments for some medical conditions.

Temperament Required

Commercial Divers should be calm and patient in their work. They should be thorough in checking each piece of equipment they plan to use. These professionals can endanger themselves if they are careless underwater. They should maintain their composure and not panic when facing danger. Divers should adapt well to changes in their working conditions. They should also enjoy spending time underwater.

Education and Training Required

The American National Standards Institute (ANSI) has established training standards for schools that have commercial diving programs. The ANSI standards require candidates to complete a combination of a minimum of 625 hours of classroom studies and practical instruction. Most commercial diving schools start training students at a beginner's level. Individuals receive a certificate of graduation after they successfully complete the course and meet the established standards. Companies that hire divers may provide additional training in the use of special equipment and procedures for these professionals.

Finances Required Before Earning

The cost of programs at commercial diving schools varies according to the length and types of courses each school offers. Schools frequently charge from $3,000 to more than $15,000 for a training program. Individuals may need to pay extra for a basic first-aid course and CPR training. They should also budget for living expenses, which can range from $5,000 to $15,000 annually. In addition, they need to pay for books, diving equipment, travel costs, and miscellaneous expenses.

Some prospective Commercial Divers take machinist, welding, or engineering courses at a career and technical school. Full-time students at public institutions usually pay between $2,000 and $7,000 a year for tuition. Private career and technical schools may charge from $4,000 to $15,000 annually for tuition. Books and supplies may cost about $1,000 per year.

Financial Aid Information

For a free booklet on financial aid, one may write to or e-mail the following:

Financial Aids for Students
Finney Company
3943 Meadowbrook Road
Minneapolis, Minnesota 55426-4505
feedback@finney-hobar.com

Attractive Features

Many Commercial Divers appreciate the challenges and variety of tasks that may accompany working underwater. People who have an adventurous nature may enjoy this career. These individuals may have opportunities to travel through their work. They may gain a sense of satisfaction from feeling that they are helping to prevent serious damage to property or protecting people's lives.

Disadvantages

Commercial Divers face a variety of dangers in their work. They risk having unexpected accidents, having their equipment fail, or encountering dangerous sea animals. Some people have health problems as a result of continual exposure to the water or extreme temperature differences. Divers are at risk for decompression sickness and other diving-related illnesses and diseases. People may have to retire from this profession if they lose their physical health.

Some people are discouraged by the amount of time they may need to spend in an entry-level position before they can achieve the income of an experienced diver. Professionals in this field may also dislike how much time they spend away from home.

Outlook for the Future

There are currently about 4,500 individuals working as Commercial Divers in the United States. Some industry experts predict the number of job opportunities for divers will likely grow as people's reliance on ocean resources increases. Other experts predict a decline in the number of positions in this field due to an increased use of remote-operated vehicles and robotics. Regardless of changes in the number of jobs, employers will probably continue to expect divers to be knowledgeable about marine applications and electronic instruments.

Licensing, Unions, Organizations

Many people enter this profession by obtaining a SCUBA diving certificate. The Association of Diving Contractors International is a trade organization that provides safety standards and certification for Commercial Divers.

Suggested Courses in High School

Students who are interested in a career as a Commercial Diver should take science classes, especially courses in chemistry, biology, and physics, through which they can learn about the underwater environment and its effects on humans. They can also benefit from taking classes in mathematics, health and safety, and industrial technology. Through physical education classes, individuals can build strength and endurance.

Suggested High School Activities

Prospective Commercial Divers can increase their physical stamina and strength by participating in sports, especially swimming activities. They can gain applicable experience for this career by taking lessons in and practicing scuba diving. Many amateur divers enjoy treasure diving, which is similar to salvage work but on a smaller scale. Students who are interested in this career can also gain experience by working on projects that require construction, welding, and mechanical skills.

Methods to Enter Work

Graduates of a diving school can contact the placement bureau of their school for assistance in finding a position in this field. They may also learn about employment opportunities by talking with other divers. In addition, employers may advertise available positions in the classified sections of newspapers or on the Internet.

Additional Information

Association of Diving Contractors International
5206 FM 1960 West, Suite 202
Houston, Texas 77069
http://www.adc-int.org

Related Web Sites

DiveWeb: Commercial Diving
http://www.diveweb.com/commdive/index.shtml
Viewers of this Web site can find article reprints from *Underwater Magazine*; diving news; and links to related associations, training facilities, and diving expeditions.

Scuba Duba: Humor & Online Magazines
http://www.scubaduba.com/humor/nfmagazine.html
This Web site offers links to diving resources worldwide. Viewers can find information about clubs, diving shops, operators, and lodging.

Testing Your Interests

How can you know if you are suited to this occupation? Ask yourself these questions. If you answer "yes" to most of them and the job sounds interesting, you may want to look into this vocation further as a possible career.

1. Do I enjoy swimming and being under water?

2. Am I in good physical condition?

3. Do I have an adventurous nature?

4. Can I be detail-oriented and meticulous when inspecting equipment?

5. Can I remain calm during dangerous situations?

Published by Finney Company, Minneapolis, Minnesota 55426-4505
© Finney Company 2005